Horizontal Double Half Hitch

Vertical Double Half Hitch

The vertical double half hitch is merely a horizonal double half hitch turned on its side. However, in the vertical double half hitch the knotting cord remains the same throughout and gets used up quickly.

The knotting cord is placed *under* the knot bearing cord and a vertical double half hitch is made. It is pushed close to the previous row of knots. The *same* knotting cord is then placed under the next knot bearing cord and "snapped" into place close to the previous row of knots. A vertical double half hitch is made around this next knot bearing cord.

Reverse Direction

Reverse Direction

Photo 1. Strip Sampler. *Helene Bress.*

The Macramé Book

Helene Bress

Flower Valley Press Gaithersburg, Maryland

*A redesigned and reissue of "The Macramé Book" by
Helene Bress originally published by Charles
Scribner's Sons, 1972.*

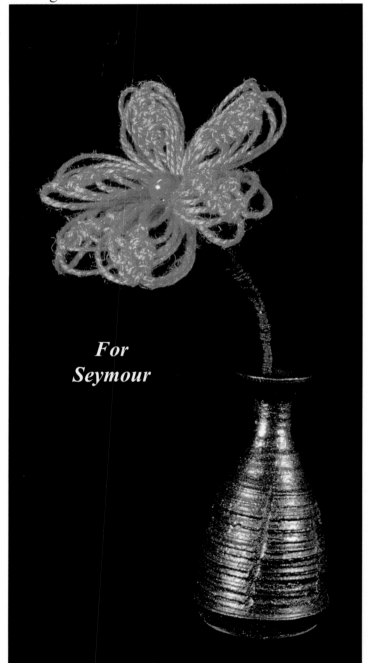

*For
Seymour*

Credits
Photography: **Allen Bress**
Knot Diagrams: **Seymour Bress**
Illustrations: **Trudy Nicholson**
Illustration on page 73: **Doramay Keasbey**

Photo 2. Marge Thurman.

Lines From a Macromaniac

I contemplate with some chagrin
the unexpected state I'm in:

When any graduate of Vassar
prefers to make an antimacassar
instead of, say, an antitoxin,
she doubltess has a head with rocks in.

My tastes had always run to yachting,
modern dance and Greek - not knotting;
I thought that Macramé was not
a piece of handwork, but a Scot.

A clod I was, a duffer whose
infrequent stabs at tying shoes
would end, with constancy uncanny,
in knots irrevocably granny.

When suddenly, with little warning,
I woke to find myself, one morning,
struck with pangs of macramania,
and growing, with each moment, zania.

I entered on a knotting binge
by ravaging my bathrobe fringe
with beaded knot and Josephine,
(It seems to me it should demean

an empress of such fame to lend
her handle to a carrick bend.)
From there I seized a clothesline, which is
now reduced to single hitches.

All things on which my hands were laid
were in an instant macraméd.
For diamond rings and furs I care not;
I ask for nothing but a square knot.

And now, in keeping with this format,
my doorstep has a knotted doormat;
my shower has a knotted curtain;
a knotted waistband keeps my shirt in.

My hair, when recently shampooed,
is settled in a knotted snood;
my knees are warmed with knotted shawls;
a knotted hanging decks the halls.

My floors are laid with knotted rugs;
my arms are wrapped in knotted shrugs;
the tassels on my shades consist
of head of Turk and monkey's fist.

I covered up the baby grand
with bullion knot and overhand.
(What other handicraft or hobby
provides one with a knotted Knabe?)

I'm hoping that in time the tide'll
change and leave my fingers idle.
Perhaps some day with luck I'll find
a man who's macramé-inclined.

And then the tie I conjure up shall
be a knot that's strictly nuptial.

- Sylvia Cassedy   1971

Acknowledgments (1972)

What is it that makes craftspeople - as a group - the great people they are? Is it their involvement in something in which they find great fulfillment?

The copious amount of cooperation, confidence, and trust that I encountered while writing this book was extraordinary. It has made it a particularly pleasant adventure for me.

Before I had written down even one word, Claribel Rathke offered to type my manuscript for me - and that was no idle offer. A pleasant, willing typist, well versed in the crafts - a perfect combination.

Thoughtfulness and helpfulness abounded. Thank you, Ellen Bennett, for the many kind things you did - so freely and cordially. Dear Martha and Dear Jeanne - I could always count on you. Whether it was encouragement, technical advice, a sounding board, or - whatever, Martha Hoering and Jeanne Vernon were always there. Among those other free spirits who saw a challenge, accepted it willingly, and solved it magnificently were Doramay Keasbey, Mary Belle Frey, and Trudy Nicholson.

A very special thank you to all of those whose work is shown in the book - and to all of those who sent photographs or lent work for us to photograph, and - alas - there was no room to show it. Your cooperation cannot be overstated.

Behind the cold, stone facades of our nation's museums are some very warm people. Those I have come in contact with are very knowlegeable as well, and very willing to share their knowledge with you. Particular thanks to Doris Bowman of the Smithsonian Institution in Washington, D.C. Thanks, too, to Grace Cooper and my other Smithsonian friends. At the Cooper-Hewitt Museum of Decorative Arts and Design, New York, my thanks go to Milton Sonday and Sandra Shaffer for their kind assistance even before their collection was properly housed in their new headquarters.

Because of her kindness and calm confidence, my editor, Elinor Parker, made this book a pleasure to write. There are many people behind the scenes at Charles Scribner's Sons. They have treated me well.

I have a very dear family - and each helped in his own way. My son Allen was my photographer. With great pride, I say that his work speaks for itself. How nice to have had a photographer on the premises. How nice to have had such a dependable and easy to work with photographer who used much good judgment and who respected the work of others - as well as his own.

My son Steven helped directly when he could and his efforts can be found in many places in this book. What can't be shown are all the very important, indirect ways in which he helped - such as apprenticing in the darkroom and respecting my need to work uninterruptedly.

My son Dan was away at college. The vibrations he sent home were of encouragement and pride.

And as for my husband, Seymour, I'm afraid words won't adequately express the contributions he made and my appreciation of them. In between his very many responsibilities, he made time to draw all the knot diagrams, and was substitute typist, substitute photographer, and full-time hand-holder. When I said "I can't," he looked at me with such sincere, utter disbelief that I began to believe "I could." He constantly supplied me with a very liberal sprinkling of that most important, undefinable something we usually refer to - as love.

Photo 3. Purse. Here's a purse that has been in Margie Thurman's family for many years. It is made of paper twine that was much in use in the early 1900's. Courtesy, *Margie Thurman.*

A Note from the Book Designer (1998)

This book is a *redesign* of "The Macramé Book" by Helene Bress, originally published by Charles Scribner's Sons in 1972. We originally planned to republish the book exactly as it had been published but we found that the original "negatives" or masters of The Macramé Book had been destroyed. At this point the job of redesigning the book was given to me.

My first task was to retype all the text from the original. Of course I typed as carefully as I could, ran everything through a spell-checker and then had two different people proofread it. However, there may be something here or there that we missed. If so, it was my fault, not a deliberate change. During the proofing process, we made some small changes to the text. These changes were grammatical, not informational. Otherwise, the revised book is identical with the original book.

After the text was in it was time to work with the photos and illustrations. My father brought boxes of photos and slides into the office. As I was going through them I found that although the original book was black and white, color slides were taken of almost all pieces. We decided that the color slides added so much to the book that we would do the entire book in color. After talking things over with our printer, we determined that the revised Macramé Book should be 160 pages. As this was 100 pages shorter than the original, the entire book was going to have to be redesigned. We decided to omit the chapter "Once Upon a Time" which covered the history of macramé and to intersperse the work of the featured artists from another chapter, "Artists At Work". Other than that the majority of the text remains intact.

The next step was to scan in all photos, slides and illustrations. The illustrations and photos were scanned on an Agfa Arcus II scanner. The original scans were made in 300 dpi, with the largest width 7.5 inches and height 10 inches. Next the slides were scanned on a Polaroid SprintScan 35. The slides were scanned in at 2700 dpi and the black point was adjusted by the scanner. The images were saved in a TIF format on CD-ROMs.

All color slides were then processed in Adobe Photoshop. First "histogram levels" were adjusted. The black and white points were moved in and the middle slider was adjusted to make the image "pop." Then the color was adjusted. I encountered problems when color adjusting because I no longer had access to the original pieces. The slides were over twenty years old, which was causing a color shift, and the films used over twenty years ago were not as color balanced as modern films. So, for a lot of the images I had to guess at the colors. If the colors are not right, it is my fault. I used the color balance sliders to adjust the images. In general I had to add a lot of yellow, take out some red and a little green. I used the "Variation" window for the more complicated adjustments. Next, I cleaned up scratches and other small imperfections. Finally I used the filter "Unsharp Mask" to sharpen the images. The thing to remember is that all the color images were digitally manipulated.

Once I had all the pieces, I started to design the book using Quark X-Press. Using modern software allowed me to easily adjust image sizes and placement. This was particularly important in Chapter Two where I was able to give the entire chapter a more useful, cleaner look. Some of the images from the original book were not used as I did not have them in color, and a few new images were added.

Happy Knotting
Dan Bress

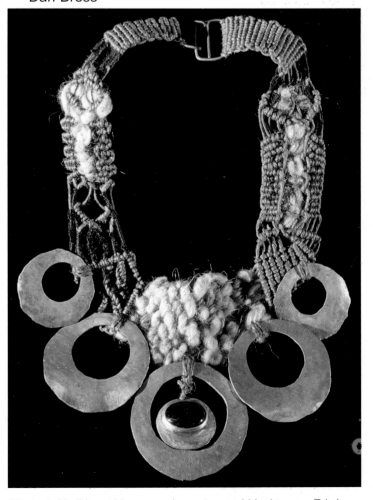

Photo 4. Necklace. Linen, wool, pewter, and black onyx. *Edwina Drobny.*

Contents

Table of Contents

Table of Contents

Photo 5. Projects #1 through #5. Once you have mastered the techniques for making these five belts, you're well into the art of macramé.

In the Beginning

Macramé is fun to do - and easy to learn. If you are a beginner, follow the first two chapters through from beginning to end and you will learn the basics, unravel the mysteries of macramé, and complete several projects as well. Happy Knotting!

Materials Needed To Begin

The materials pictured are good to start with.

Knotting Board. The knotting board should be firm, yet allow pins to penetrate. The two pictured are readily available and work very successfully.

Polyurethane (plastic foam) Kneeling Pad, Pillow or Pillow Form. A convenient size is about 12" x 16". The kneeling pad is available in hardware stores; the pillow or pillow form wherever pillows are sold: variety stores, department stores, fabric stores, etc.

Insulating Board. Available from lumberyards. Sometimes scraps are sold; often a large sheet must be bought and cut to size.

If the above are not available, look on pages 59 to 60 for some substitutes.

Sturdy Pins. Have on hand about two dozen.

"T" pins or "Wig" pins are good for use with either type of knotting board. If you can't find them with sewing supplies, try the department where hair accessories are sold.

"U" pins or "Tidy" pins work very well with plastic foam knotting boards. These are most often found on sewing and notions counters.

Cord or twine. For the first few projects seine twine #18 or #21 is most desirable and most readily available. It's generally obtainable in hardware stores and hardware departments of department stores. Other sizes work well, too. If you cannot get seine twine, some good substitutes are jute, polypropylene rug yarn, or any strong, hard twisted cord you may have.

Rubber Bands, Scissors, Ruler, Tracing Paper.

Photo 6. Supplies

To Begin: Overhand Knot

A very useful knot to know is the overhand knot. You've probably tied it hundreds of times before for various purposes.

Let's begin by practicing this simple knot.

The only material you need in order to learn and practice this one is an 18-inch cord made of any material.

To make the overhand knot:

Near one end, make a loop over the cord.

Bring the end under the cord, and through the loop.

Pull taut.

One overhand knot is completed. It's not a thing of beauty in itself, but will have many uses.

For practice, repeat the knot all along the cord. Spacing, at this time, is not important.

Photo 7. Neckpiece. *Paul Johnson.*

Square Knot

One of the very basic knots in macramé is the square knot. Let's learn this knot by making a little sample.

Materials needed

Seine twine #18 or #21, or jute. Cut 4 cords 2 feet long.

Tie an overhand knot in each cord about 1 1/2 inches from one end.

Put a pin though each overhand knot and pin each cord onto your knotting board. The knots should be touching each other.

The two central cords are stationary core cords. They may be pinned down near the bottom of the knotting board, if desired.

To do the square knot:

Take the cord on the right (cord 4) and place it over and to the left of the two central cords. Drop cord 4.

Take the cord on the left (cord 1) and place it on top of cord 4. (The figure you have now made resembles a backwards 4.)

Bring cord 1 under the two central cords and through the loop on the right.

Bring cord 1 under the two central cords, and through the loop on the left.

Tighten by pulling on cords 1 and 4.

Pull firmly - but not with all your strength. The first half of the square knot is completed and should be just below the overhand knots.

Tighten with cords 1 and 4.

One square knot is now completed.

The second half of the square knot is the same as the first, but in reverse.

Cord 4 is now on the left. Bring it over and to the right of the two central cords. Drop cord 4.

After making several knots, a rhythm will begin to emerge.

First half:
Start with the right cord:

Right **Over** central cords
Left   **Over** cord 4
       Under central cords
and   **Thru** loop

Second half:
Start with the left cord:

Left   **Over** central cords
Right **Over** cord 1
       Under central cords
and   **Thru** loop.

Briefly:
Over, Over, Under and Through
Over, Over, Under and Through

Place cord 1 on top of cord 4.

Continue making square knots until the knotting cords become too short to handle easily. You will now have a row, or sennit,* of square knots measuring about 4 inches. The knotting cords will be quite short, and the two central cords quite long. There is a great deal of take-up in knotting cords, and practically none with the core cords.

For more practice, mount some more cords or continue by making the next project.

Square Knot Project #1
Sash with Square Knots

Materials needed: Seine twine #18 or #21, or jute. Amount needed: 17 yards. Beads are optional for this project. If used, 12 are needed. Holes must be large enough for the cords to go through.

To prepare:
Cut 4 cords 2 yards long.
Cut 2 cords 4 1/2 yards long.

Make an overhand knot in each cord - about 20 inches from one end.

Pin the shorter cords onto the board first. Then pin the long cords on either side of the shorter cords. The overhand knots should be touching.

You will be knotting with the two outer cords *only*. Shorten them and secure with a rubber band.

Starting from about 18 inches below the overhand knot, wind the cord around your palm, always placing the cord alongside the previous cord and working out toward your fingertips. When you have completely wound the cord, slip it off your hand and place a rubber band around the center. If the winding was done carefully, the cord will release easily as the knotting progresses. If done carelessly, you'll have to undo it occasionally and rewrap.

Leave the four central core cords dangling straight down, or pin them to the bottom of the knotting board. You will not be knotting with these. You'll be knotting around these core cords. In the sampler, you knotted around two core cords. In this project, you'll knot around four core cords.

Knotting:
Take the two outside cords and make a square knot.

Continue making square knots, one below the other until the sennit measures four inches.

Put a pin 1 1/2 inches below the last square knot.

Make a square knot and tighten it just below the pin.

Continue making square knots until four more inches are completed.

Skip a space of 1 1/2 inches as before.

Note: When the knotting nears the bottom of the board, unpin it and move it up to a more comfortable knotting height.

Repeat the above directions until the square knot sections just about circle your waist.

Make overhand knots on each cord, including the core cords, just below the last square knot.

Trim the cords until they all measure 20 inches from the overhand knots.

To finish:

If you are not using beads
Make overhand knots near the end of each cord.

If you are using beads
Slip a bead onto the end of one of the 20 inch strands.

Make an overhand know below the bead to keep it from falling off.

Repeat the above two steps for each 20 inch strand on both ends of your belt.

One project completed! Different spacings, different yarns, and more or fewer beads will give you a belt that is quite distinct from this one.

* A sennit is a vertical series of like knots, as, for example, a square knot sennit.

Photo 8.
Project 1.

4

Square Knot Project #2
Alternating Square Knot Sash

Materials needed:
Seine twine #18 or #21, or jute. Amount needed: 48 yards. Substitute yarns are listed on pages 68 and 69. Beads are optional. If used, 24 are needed. Holes must be large enough for the cord to go through.

To prepare:
Cut twelve cords 4 yards long.

Tie an overhand knot about 20 inches from the end of each cord.

Pin each cord to the knotting board and have each knot touching the next.

Shorten each cord and secure it with a rubber band.

This belt will be worked using groups of four cords throughout. The two outer cords of each group will be used to knot around the two core cords of that group.

Knotting:
Take the first four cords: 1, 2, 3, 4.

Using these cords, make a sennit of five square knots.

Repeat this with the next four cords: 5, 6, 7, 8.

Same with the last four cords: 9, 10, 11, 12.

Now we'll join the three rows.
Put aside the first two cords: cords 1 and 2.

Take the next four cords: 3, 4, 5, 6.

Using these four cords, tie two square knots one below the other.

Take the next four cords: 7, 8, 9, 10.

Using those cords, tie two square knots. There will be two cords left over on the right side: 11, 12.

Now to regroup:
Pick up cords 1, 2, 3, 4.

Make a sennit of five square knots with those four cords.

Do the same with cords 5, 6, 7, and 8.

Same with cords 9, 10, 11, and 12.

Keep alternating the square knot sections until the knotted portion fits almost completely around your waist.

To finish:
Tie an overhand knot on each cord just below the last square knot, then finish as in Square Knot Project #1.

Photo 9. Project 2. Alternating Square Knot Sash.

Double Half Hitch

The two knots most basic to macramé are the square knot, which you now know, and the double half hitch. The double half hitch can be made horizontally, vertically, diagonally, and in a straight or curved line. To learn the double half hitch, let's make another sample.

Materials needed: Seine twine #18 or #21, or jute.

To prepare:
Cut eight cords - each cord 2 feet long.
    Make an overhand knot in each cord, about 1fi inches from one end.
    Pin the cords to your knotting board side by side. Put one pin through the center of each overhand knot and pin them to the board so that the knots are touching each other.

To Knot:
Place a pin between cord 1 and cord 2.
    Bring cord 1 on top of all the other cords and place it just below the line of overhand knots. Cord 1 will now be used as a knot bearer.
    Hold the knot bearer (cord 1) horizontally with your right hand.
    With your left hand, pick up cord 2.
    **Bring cord 2 up, and on top of the knot bearer.
    (Keep the knotting cord well over to the right to avoid getting tangled in the pins.)
    Bring it under the knot bearer and
    Through the loop it formed.
    Pull cord 2 taut while pushing it close to the pins. **
    Half the knot has been formed.
    With the same cord (cord 2) repeat the steps between the asterisks.
    Be sure the knots are standing vertically and are pushed close to the overhand knots before tightening the cord. One complete double half hitch has been made.
    Continue knotting this way with the rest of the cords across the row.

To return:

Double half hitch from right to left.

Cord 1 will still be used as your knot bearer.

Bring the knot bearer over to the left and on top of all the other cords.

Hold knot bearer with your left hand. Keep it close to and parallel to the previous row of knots.

With your right hand pick up cord 8.

**Bring it on top of knot bearer. (Keep the knotting cord well over to the left to avoid getting tangled in the pins.)

Take cord 8 under the knot bearer and through the loop you've formed.

Push it close to the previous row of knots and pull it taut.**

With the same cord (cord 8) repeat the steps between the asterisks using cords 7 through 2 in turn.

Repeat rows 1 and 2.

When you have completed four rows, you will begin to be comfortable with the double half hitch. Now we're going to use this same knot in a slightly different way - and will form an angle.

Trace the pattern for angles onto a piece of paper. Pin the paper pattern onto your knotting board so that the arrow touches the bottom right corner of your knotting. Choose as your guide for angling the line on the pattern which is closest to cord 1. Cord 1 will be your knot bearer again.

Place a pin between cords 1 and 2.

Bring cord 1 on top of all the other cords and place it at an angle this time. Choose as your guide the line of the paper pattern which is closest to cord 1.

Hold the knot bearer firmly with your right hand, remembering to keep the knot bearer at the proper angle.

Double half hitch as before, with cord 2 through 8, keeping the knot bearer at an angle.

To return, place a pin between cord 8 and the knot bearer.

Bring the knot bearer to the left and on top of all the other cords.

Hold the knot bearer with your left hand along the same pattern line you have been following.

Double half hitch along the knot bearer, using cords 8 through 2.

Continue as above one or two more times.

The sash on the next page uses this technique.

Angle Chart may be enlarged or made smaller on a photocopy machine.

Photo 10. Bell Pull by Ella Bolster

Photo 11. One section of a Strip Sampler, *Helene Bress.*

Sash Using Double Half Hitch
Project #3

Materials needed: Seine twine #18 or #21, or jute.
Amount needed: 30 yards. Substitute yarns are listed
on pages 68 and 69.

To prepare:
Cut ten cords, each cord three yards long. Place each
cord in a separate pile so that they won't tangle.

Take one cord and tie an overhand knot about 20
inches from one end.

Put a pin through the overhand knot and pin it to
the knotting board.

Shorten the cord.

Repeat the same steps for each of the remaining
cords.

Pin the cords side by side as on the sampler.

Cord 1 will be your knot bearer throughout this
project.

To knot:
Start by making two rows of horizontal double half
hitches, as in the sample.

Pin the paper pattern you used for your sample
under your knotting as before. This will again be
used as a guide for angling.

Bring the knot bearer on top of the other cords
and place it at an angle. Use as your guide the line
on the paper pattern which is closest to cord 1.

Double half hitch with cords 2 through 10.

Place a pin between cord 10 and the knot bearer.

Angle knot bearer to the left, on top of the other
cords.

Double half hitch with cords 10 through 2.

Continue to angle to the right and left until the
sash just about meets around your waist.

Now make two more rows of horizontal double
half hitches.

To Finish:
Remove the overhand knots from the beginning of the
sash. The sash will now have ten strands hanging at
each end. On each strand make about four or five
overhand knots at irregular intervals, as in the picture.

Photo 12. Project #3. Sash using double half
stitches. Overhand knots at irregular intervals form
the endings of this sash.

Diamond Belt
Project #4

Materials needed:
Seine twine #18 or #21, or jute. Amount needed: 36 yards. Two rings - "O" or "D" rings - about 1 1/2 inches in size (See page 73.) Substitute yarns are listed on pages 68 and 69. If heavier yarns are used, larger rings may be needed.

To Prepare:
Pin the two rings to the board.
   Cut one cord six yards long.
   Fold that cord in half.
   Place the folded half - the end with the loop - on top of, around, and behind the rings.
   Take the cut ends of the cord and slip them through the loop in the cord.
   Pull the ends tight.
   Detailed drawings of this are on page 49.
   Shorten each end of the cords separately.

Repeat the above with five more cords.
   You now have 12 working cords on your rings and each cord is three yards long.
   Do two rows of double half hitches, as in the previous project, but keep the knots close to the rings. This will keep the rings firmly in place.

Photo 13. Project #4. Beginning and ending of the Diamond Belt.

Trace or photocopy the diamond pattern onto a piece of paper. Pin this pattern to the board so that the point of the diamond is between cords 6 and 7.

Divide your cords in half. Put the first six cords aside to the left, and work with the six cords on the right.

Cord 7 will be your knot bearer for this part.

1. Angle to the right using cords 8 through 12 in order.

2. Place a pin between the knot bearer (cord 7) and cord 12. Angle back, using cords 12 through 8 in order. Use as your guide that line on the pattern closest to cord 7 where it begins to angle back.

3. Now put these cords aside and go back to those you set aside before. Cord 6 will be your knot bearer for this side.

Angle to the left, using cords 5 through 1 in order.

4. Place a pin between the knot bearer (cord 6) and cord 1. Angle back to the right, using cords 1 through 5 in order.

Both knot-bearing cords are now back in the center. To close the diamond they form:

5. Take cord 7 and place it on top of cord 6.

6. With cord 6, double half hitch over cord 7.

7. Cord 7 now becomes the holding cord for the left part of the diamond, and cord 6 now becomes the holding cord for the right part of the diamond.

Continue making diamonds as above until the belt is a few inches longer than your waist.

To finish:

Make overhand knots just below the last row of double half hitches. Trim the cords so that they're about half an inch long.

Photo 14. Chart for Diamonds may be made larger or smaller on a photocopy machine.

Photo 15. Necklace. *Paul Johnson.*

Diamond Belt with Variations
Project #5

Materials needed:

Seine twine #18 or #21, or jute. Amount needed: 56 yards. Buckle 1 1/2 inches - 2 inches wide. Substitute yarns are listed on pages 68 and 69. If using other yarns, use any buckle that will hold 14 cords comfortably.

To Prepare:

Cut seven cords, each cord 8 yards long.

Fold each cord in half and mount it onto the bar of your buckle the same way you mounted cords on the rings in the previous project.

You will now have 14 cords and each cord will be four yards long. Use the paper pattern you made for the previous project. Pin it to your board with the point of the diamond between cords 7 and 8. Your middle cords, cords 7 and 8, are knot bearers.

Diamond #1

Make one complete diamond as in the previous project.

Diamond #2

Continue by making a second diamond, but make only the top half of it.

Now work with the four central cords (5, 6, 9, 10). Cords 5 and 10 will be the knotting cords; cords 6 and 9 will be the stationary core cords.

Using the four central cords, make a sennit of square knots. When you reach the center of the diamond, count the number of knots needed to get to that point. Make the same number for the bottom half of the sennit.

Finish the bottom of the diamond.

Diamond #3

Make the top half of diamond #3.

Put the two knot-bearing cords aside.

Make a square knot, using cords 1 and 14. Knot these cords around all the remaining cords.

Do not draw the square knot in too tightly; do not tighten it so much that the diamond draws in.

Make the bottom half of the diamond, using the cords in the same order as they come from the top half of the diamond.

Photo 16. Project #5. Belt. Diamonds with Variations. The beginning and end of the belt are shown.

Diamond #4   Alternating Square Knots

Make the top half of the next diamond.

Row 1: Make a square knot with the four central cords (cords 5, 6, 9, and 10).

Row 2: Alternate the square knots and make two square knots in this row - one with cords 3, 4, 5, 6, the other with cords 9, 10, 11, and 12.

Row 3: Alternate again. Three square knots will be made in this row - one with cords 1, 2, 3, 4, one with cords 5, 6, 9, 10, and one with cords 11, 12, 13, and 14.

The two knot-bearing cords will not be used for making any square knots.

Row: 4 Knot the same as you did row 2.

Row 5: Knot the same as you did row 1.

Make the bottom half of the diamond.

Repeat these four diamonds until the belt goes almost completely around your waist. Then do a few more diamonds with alternating square knots so that the buckle "tongue" will have a hole to go through.

To Finish:

Work on the back side of the belt. With a crochet hook or a large-eyed embroidery needle, pull each end through two knots. Make an overhand knot as close to the belt as possible. Clip the end short. If desired, glue the ends down, and if the belt will be washed, use a glue that is not water soluble.

Variations of the previous belts are easy to design. Different materials, the use of color, different spacings, using the knots in a different order, are all ways of varying the original theme.

Once you feel secure with the basic knots and the variations presented in this chapter, you have graduated from the beginner stage.

The following chapters of this book are intended to present new material, answer questions and, most hopefully, to inspire.

Chapter Two

Photo 17. Strip Sampler by Helene Bress.

Themes and Variations

Now that you know the basics of macramé, the door is wide open. You can close the door on the first chapter, and just refer to the remaining chapters from now on. The basic knots are reviewed; some new ones are added for you to learn at your convenience. We'll try to help you resolve your problems and free you to create your own projects.

Terms Used in Macramé

- Mounting Piece
- Sennit of Square Knots
- Knotting Cord
- Core Cord

Photo 18. Turkey Red Owl 1971. Paul Johnson has interpreted this very special breed of owl in his own fanciful way. Hand-dyed jute. 9" x 14". *Paul Johnson.*

- Mounting Piece
- Knotting Cord
- Knot-Bearing Cord

1. Sennit of Square Knots

One square knot is made directly below the next.

Courtesy of
Jonathan Bress.

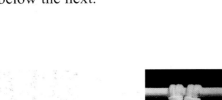

3. Square Knot Sennit with Spaces

A sennit of square knots was made. A pin was placed below the fourth knot. A square knot was made below the pin and tightened right beneath the pin.

5. Square Knot Sennit with Knotting Cords and Core Cords Switching Positions for an Interesting Color and Design Effect

2. Sennit of Square Knots Using One Light-Colored Knotting Cord and One Dark Knotting Cord

The colors are reversed on the other side of the sennit.

4. Two-Color Square Knot Sennit with Bead

The bead was slipped onto the two core cords and pushed up into place. More knots were made below it.

6. Two-Color Square Knot Sennit with Overhand Knots

As in this sennit, a second color can be hidden within a sennit and brought to the surface at will. In this case, an overhand knot accentuates the second color.

7. Square Knot Sennit with Overhand Knot Variations

9. Two-Color, Six-Strand Square Knot Sennit

Four square knots were made using the two outside cords as knotting cords and the remaining four cords as core cords. The sennit was then split into two parts, with two light-colored cords and one dark-colored cord in each part. Using the light cords as knotting cords, three more square knots were formed with each group. The darker cord was then used to make an overhand knot.

10. Square Knot Sennit with Overhand Knots at the Edges of Every Other Square Knot

8. Two-Color Square Knot Sennit with Overhand Knot and Bead

The bead adds a third color to this sennit.

1 2 3 4 5 6

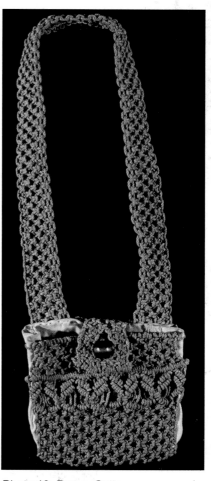

Photo 19. Purse. Cotton, canvas and wood.

Spirals

A spiral is made by repeating the first half of the square knot over, and over, and over again until the desired length is made. The only trick is this: after you have made a few half square knots (about four or five), you will notice that the sennit has begun to twist and is almost facing your knotting board. Allow the knotting cords to continue going in the direction in which they are headed and help them along. Bring the top knotting cord over to the side to which it is pointing. Bring the bottom knotting cord under the core cords and to the opposite side. Now continue making half square knots exactly as you had been before. After a few more half knots have been made, the spiraling action will repeat itself.

12. Spiral Sennit of Half Square Knots

This sennit twists in the direction opposite to the first one because it is made with the second half of the square knot repeated over and over again.

14. Spiral Sennit with Beads

11. Spiral Sennit of Half Square Knots

The first half of the square knot (as described on pages 2-4) was made over and over again.

13. Spiral Sennit Interrupted with Bands of Whole Square Knot Sennits

15. Spiral Sennit with Direction of Twist Changing After Four Half Square Knots

Four half square knots were made using the first half of the square knot, then four were made using the second half of the square knot. This was repeated throughout.

16. Spiral Sennit with Direction of the Twist Changing After Seven Half Square Knots

17. Spiral Sennit with Direction of Twist Changing After Fifteen Half Square Knots

Square Knot Variations

18. Square Knot Sennit with Picots

Place a pin a distance below the second square knot of the sennit. Make a square knot or two below the pin. Remove the pin, and slide the square knots close to the previous knots. The slack cords between the square knots will now bow out. If several picots are to be made, graph paper will be a helpful guide for spacing the pins.

19. Square Knot Sennit with Picots of Graduated Sizes

Increase or decrease the distance of the pin beneath the square knots to get picots of varying sizes.

20. Six-Strand Square Knot Sennit Using Only Two Core Cords and Two Knotting Cords at One Time

First, cords 2 and 5 were used as knotting cords and two square knots were made. Then, cords 1 and 6 were used and two square knots were made.

21. Alternating Square Knot Band: One and One

Four cords, two knotting cords and two core cords, were used for each square knot throughout this sample.

Row 1: One square knot was made with each group of four cords:

Cords 1, 2, 3 and 4 were used for the first square knot;

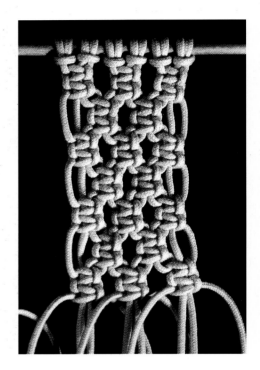

Cords 5, 6, 7, and 8 were used for the second square knot; Cords 9, 10, 11, and 12 were used for the third square knot.

Row 2: The first two cords were put aside.

The next four cords (cords 3, 4, 5, and 6) were used to make a square knot. Then, the next four cords (cords 7, 8, 9, and 10) were used to make a square knot. The last two cords were not used in this row.

Row 3: Same as Row 1.

Row 4: Same as Row 2.

The same pattern was repeated throughout.

22. Alternating Square Knot Band: Two and Two

The same groupings of the cords were used in this sample, but two square knots were made with each set of cords instead of one. Many more variations of this sort are possible.

23. Alternating Square Knots with an Open, Net-like Effect

The same technique is used as in the previous samples, but spaces are left between the knots. To keep the spaces even, graph paper can be pinned to your knotting board and pins placed just above the point where the knots are to be made. The knots are then made below the pins. Or, the knots can be formed around an appropriate sized implement, such as a dowel or ruler.

24. A Pattern of Alternating Square Knots Using Two Colors

25. Alternating Square Knots with Knotting and Core Cords Changing Places

26. Alternating Square Knots and a Cross-over of Square Knot Sennits

Variations with Double Half Hitches

28. Rows of Horizontal Double Half Hitches

27. Square Knot Sennit with Raised Picots

29. Rows of Horizontal Double Half Hitches with Spaces In Between

A sennit of square knots was made. A little space was left and four more square knots were made. Each core cord was threaded onto a large-eyed yarn needle. The core cords were brought up and then put through the space left between the square knots. The core cords were pulled tight and a raised picot was formed. More square knots were made directly below the raised picot.

1 2 3 4

2
3

1   4

30. Diagonal Double Half Hitches

The holding cord is held at an angle and double half hitches are knotted onto it. It's helpful to pin guide lines to your knotting board so that the angles you form will be even. (There is a more complete description in Chapter 1.)

31. Diagonal Double Half Hitches to Form a Diamond

The two center cords (cords A and B) are the knot-bearing cords.

Photo 20. Belt. *Melissa Diamanti.*

32. One Diamond Completed and Another Started

The point at which the diamonds cross is flat and neat. When the two knot-bearing cords have both reached the center of the diamond, place cord A over cord B. Take cord B and make a double half hitch onto cord A.

Cord A now becomes the knot bearer for the right side of the next diamond and cord B becomes the knot bearer for the left side of the next diamond.

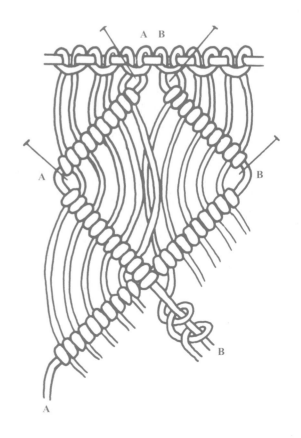

33. X's Made with Double Half Hitches

For X's, the first and last cord are the knot bearers.

34. Double Diamonds with Double Half Hitches

The two center cords (6 and 7) are the knot bearers for the first row of the diamond. The cords on either side of this (cords 5 and 8) become the knot bearers for the second row of the diamond. These same cords (cords 5 and 8) remain the knot bearers for the next row. Cords 6 and 7 then become the knot bearers for the fourth row, which completes the double diamond.

35. Diamond Variation

The two center cords (6 and 7) are knot bearers for the first row; 5 and 8 for the second row; 4 and 9 for the third row. Cords 4 and 9 continue as knot bearers to complete the diamond.

36. Double Half Hitch Variation

Row 1: Cords 6 and 7 are knot bearers and all the other cords are hitched onto them. These knot bearers are now set aside and not used for the rest of the motif.

Row 2: Cords 5 and 8 are now knot bearers and all the cords, except 6 and 7 are hitched onto them. These knot bearers are set aside and not used for the rest of the motif.

Row 3: Cords 4 and 9 are knot bearers, and all the cords, except 5, 6 7, and 8, are knotted onto it. These knot bearers are set aside and not used for the rest of the motif.

Row 4: Cords 3 and 10 are knot bearers, and the same knotting pattern as above is followed.

Row 5: Cords 2 and 11 are knot bearers. The same knotting pattern as above is followed.

Fanciful Variations

37. Diamond with Square Knot Acting as a Gathering Knot

The top half of the diamond is formed in the usual manner. The two knot-bearing cords (cords 6 and 7) are now put aside and are not used while the square knot is being made. The two outside cords (cords 1 and 12) are picked up and are used to make a square knot using the cords remaining within the diamond as core cords. So as not to distort the diamond shape, the square knot is not pulled in too taut.

The bottom half of the diamond is now made in the usual manner. For a graceful effect, hitch the cords onto the bottom half in the same order as they come from the top part of the diamond.

38. Diamond with Alternating Square Knots

The top half of the diamond is formed in the usual manner. The two knot-bearing cords are put aside, and are not used to make the center pattern. Starting with the four center cords, a square knot is made. The pattern of alternating square knots is continued:
2 knots in the second row
3 knots in the third row
2 knots in the fourth row
1 knot in the fifth row.
Then the knot-bearing cords are angled back to the center, and the diamond is completed.

39. Diamond with Square Knot Sennit and Bead

The top half of the diamond is made in the usual manner. With the four central cords, a square knot sennit with a bead is made. The bottom half of the diamond is then completed.

40. Diamond with a Spiral and Square Knots

Fourteen cords are used this time, and the top half of the diamond is completed in the usual manner. The two knot-bearing cords are put aside. A spiral of half knots is made down the center and one square knot is made on either side of it. Notice that the two square knots are mirror images of one another. One is made in the conventional way. In the other, the knotting sequence is reversed.

41. Diamond Variation

The top half of the diamond is formed in the usual manner. The knot-bearing cord on the left (cord 6) is then angled back toward the center and the knotting cords from the top right half of the diamond are now hitched onto it: first cord 8, then 9, 10, 11, and 12. The other half of the diamond is done in the same manner.

42. Diamond Variation

The top half of the diamond is formed in the usual manner. Then the knot-bearing cord on the right (cord 7) is angled back to the center and the knotting cords are hitched on in this order: cord 8 first, 9 next, then 10, 11, and 12. The knot bearing cord on the left (cord 6) is then angled back to the center, and the knotting cords are hitched on in this order: 5, 4, 3, 2, and 1.

43. Weaving within a Diamond

Again, the top half of the diamond is formed in the usual manner. The cords within the diamond are then woven in this way. One at a time, the cords on the right are woven over and under the cords on the left. First, cord 8 weaves over and under cords 5, 4, 3, 2, and 1. Cord 8 is pushed up close to the side of the diamond. Next, cord 9 weaves under and over cord 5, 4, 3, 2, and 1, and is then pushed close to the previous one. These steps are repeated with cords 10, 11, and 12. The bottom half of the diamond is then completed.

44. Double Diamond with Two over Two Weaving in Center

You need an even number of cords in the center to weave like this. The method is the same as for "Weaving within a Diamond" (left).

45. Shaping with Double Half Hitches

A piece can be shaped with double half hitches by changing the direction of the knot-bearing cord. Follow the lines in the picture to determine how the shape of the sample was made. With this technique, circles and other shapes are possible.

46. Pattern with Diagonal Double Half Hitches

For the first part, every sixth cord is a knot bearer. The knot bearer is angled to the left and the cords above it are hitched onto it. Then, the third cord from the top of each motif is used as a knot bearer and angles to the right. The cords above the knot bearer are hitched onto them.

Photo 21. Belt. Close up of Photo 52, page 76. *Ella Bolster.*

47. Flower Shape with Double Half Hitches

For a rounded effect, the knot-bearing cords are gently curved as the other cords are hitched onto them. Cord 1 is curved to the right and the next seven cords (2 through 8) are hitched onto it.

Cord 2 is curved over to the right and the next seven cords are hitched onto it in order (cords 3, 4, 5, 6, 7, 8, and 1).

Cord 16 is curved to the left and cords 15 through 9 are hitched onto it.

Cord 15 is curved over to the left and is used to complete the top half of the flower shape and to begin the bottom part.

All the cords are hitched onto cord 15 in the order in which they come from the top.

Cord 1 curves over to the left and the cords above it are hitched onto it.

Cord 2 curves over to the right bottom and the cords above it are hitched onto it.

Cord 16 curves over to the right and the cords above it are hitched onto it.

Angling

48. Angling with Horizontal Double Half Hitches

A whole section of knotwork can be made to shift position in this way.

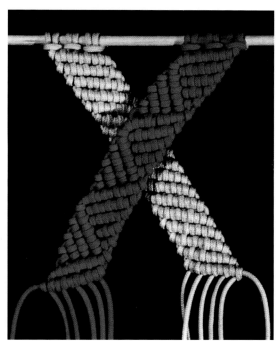

Row 1: Using cord 1 as a knot bearer, double half hitch from left to right using the rest of the cords.
Row 2: Using cord 2 as a knot bearer, double half hitch from left to right using all the cords in the previous row.
Row 3 and on: Continue in this same manner.
As you progress from one row to the next, shift your pin over to the right a bit.

Photo 22. Playing with Angles. *Helene Bress.*

49. Angling with Horizontal Double Half Hitches, Using Vertical Double Half Hitches for Textural Contrast

Row 1: Using cord 6 as a knot bearer, double half hitch from right to left, using cords 5, 4, 3, 2, and 1 in order.

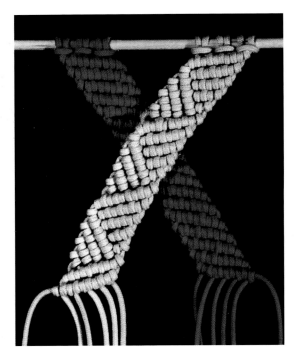

Row 2: Using cord 5 as a knot bearer, double half hitch from right to left using cords 4, 3, 2, and 1 *only*.
Row 3: Using cord 4 as a knot bearer, double half hitch from right to left using cords 3, 2, and 1 *only*.
Row 4: Using cord 3 as a knot bearer, hitch on cords 2 and 1 *only*.
Row 5: Using cord 2 as a knot bearer, hitch on cord 1 *only*.
Five cords are now just hanging on the left.
Go back to row 1 and bring cord 6 straight down, on top of the other cords.
Going from top to bottom, vertical half hitch cords 5, 4, 3, and 2 onto it.
Bring cord 5 down, and vertical half hitch cords 4, 3, and 2 onto it.
Bring cord 4 down, and vertical half hitch cords 3 and 2 onto it.
Bring cord 3 down, and vertical half hitch cord 2 onto it.
One section is now completed. Repeat this as many times as desired.

50. Angling Back and Forth with Horizontal Double Half Hitches

Row 1: Using cord 6 as a knot bearer, double half hitch from right to left using cords 5, 4, 3, 2, and 1.

Row 2: Using cord 5 as a knot bearer, double half hitch from right to left using all the cords from the previous row.

Row 3: Using cord 4 as a knot bearer, continue as before.

For this sample, continue in this manner until nine rows are completed.

Row 10: In this row, be particularly careful to keep the knots close to the knots in the previous row. Using the first cord on the left as a knot bearer (the same cord as was used as a knot bearer in the previous row), double half hitch from left to right using all the cords in the previous row.

Row 11: using the first cord that is now on the left double half hitch from left to right, using all the cords from the previous row.

Row 12 and on: Continue in this same manner.

51. Angling with Horizontal Double Half Hitches, using Vertical Double Half Hitches for a Textural Change

Rows 1 through 5: As in sample 48.
Rows 6 through 9: As in sample 49, with the shaping going in the opposite direction.
The bottom half angles back as on the top of sample 50, and ends as in sample 49.

52. Angling and Shaping with Horizontal Double Half Hitches and Sennits of Square Knots

The first six rows angle to the right. The cords are separated and two sennits of square knots are made. The cords are joined again and the pattern angles to the left.

53. Angling and Shaping with Horizontal Double Half Hitches and Alternating Square Knots.

The first six rows angle to the left. A pattern of alternating square knots is inserted. The last six rows then angle to the right.

54. Angling with Horizontal Double Half Hitches (Variation)

The light-colored section of this band was made by angling with horizontal double half hitches first to the right, then left, then right, then left again. The dark-colored section was angled first to the left, then right, left, and right again. The two sections were then overlapped and intertwined.

55. Shell Knot Button Using Square Knots and Double Half Hitches. Eight Cord Method

Row 1: One square knot is made with the first four cords; one square knot with the last four cords.
Row 2: Cord 5 is now used as a knot bearer. Bring it over to the left and hold it at an angle. Double half hitch cords 4, 3, 2, and 1 onto it.
Row 3: Cord 6 is now used as a knot bearer. Bring it over to the left, just below the previous row. Double half hitch cords 4, 3, 2, and 1 onto it.
Rows 4 and 5: Repeat the above with cords 7 and 8 as knot bearers.
Row 6: Make a sennit of square knots with cords 1, 2, 3, and 4. Make a second sennit of square knots with cords 5, 6, 7, and 8.
Rows 7 through 10: Repeat steps 2 through 5 to make another shell knot button.

To Complete the Shell Knot Button:
Row 11: Make a square knot with cords 1, 2, 3, and 4. Make a square knot with cords 5, 6, 7, and 8.

56. Shell Knot Button with Decorative Insert of Chain Knots

Rows 1 through 5: Repeat the first five steps in number 55.

Row 6: Make one square knot with the first four cords and another square knot with the second four cords. This completes one shell knot button.

Row 7 and on: Make four single chain sennits below the square knots and end with another shell knot button.

57. Shell Knot Button Made with Ten Cords

Cords 5 and 6 will be your knot bearers.

1. Curve cord 5 over to the left and down a little. Double half hitch cords 4, 3, 2, and 1 onto it.
2. Curve cord 6 over to the right and down a little. Double half hitch cords 7, 8, 9, and 10 onto it. For the time being, put both of these knot bearers aside.
3. Make a square knot with cords 1, 2, 3, and 4.
4. Make a square knot with cords 7, 8, 9, and 10.
5. Using cord 7 as a new knot bearer, double half hitch cords 4, 3, 2, and 1 onto it.
6. Using cord 8 as a new knot bearer, double half hitch cords 4, 3, 2, and 1 onto it.
7. Using cord 9 as a new knot bearer, double half hitch cords 4, 3, 2, and 1 onto it.

8. Using cord 10 as a new knot bearer, double half hitch cords 4, 3, 2, and 1 onto it.
9. Make a *very tight* square knot with cords 1, 2, 3, and 4.
10. Make a *very tight* square knot with cords 7, 8, 9, and 10.

You will now use the knot bearers you put aside before.

11. Curve cord 6 to the left and center. Double half hitch cords 4, 3, 2, and 1 onto it.
12. Curve cord 5 to the right and center. Double half hitch cords 7, 8, 9, and 10 onto it.

The two center cords are crossed as diamonds are crossed.

Vertical Double Half Hitches

58. Vertical Double Half Hitches with Picots

The vertical double half hitch is shown on 000. To make the picot, place a pin a distance away from the last edge knot. Bring the knotting cord around the pin, and continue knotting back along the next row.

59. Vertical Double Half Hitches with Exaggerated Picots or Swirls

Three separate knotting cords are used for this.
Row 1: Pin a knotting cord (cord A) to the knotting board and make vertical half hitches across the row from left to right.
Row 2: Pin a second knotting cord (cord B) to the knotting board and make vertical half hitches across the row from left to right.
Row 3: Pin a third knotting cord of a darker color (cord C) to the knotting board and again make vertical half hitches across the row from left to right.
Row 4: Using the same knotting cord as you used for Row 3 (cord C), make a small picot and vertical half hitch across the row from right to left.
Row 5: Put a pin farther to the right of the knotting to make a larger picot than before. With cord B vertical half hitch across the row from right to left.
Row 6: Put a pin still further to the right than the last one. With cord A, vertical half hitch across the row from right to left.

60. Vertical Double Half Hitches with Some Unknotted Area

Using cord 1 as a knotting cord, two rows of vertical half hitches were made. The knotting was continued over the first two cords only. Then cord 8 was picked up and used as a knotting cord for vertical half hitches on the last two cords. Cord 8 was brought back to its original position and dropped. Cord 1 was used as a knotting cord again and vertical half hitches were made across the entire row.

Cavandoli

61. Cavandoli Stitch

A combination of vertical and horizontal double half hitches in two colors are used to form a design. The light-colored background is made of horizontal double half hitches; the darker design areas are made of vertical double half hitches. Ten light-colored cords were hitched onto the dowel. A separate, extra-long, dark-colored cord was cut, pinned to the knotting board and used alternately as a knot bearer and as a knotting cord.

For the horizontal half hitches, the dark cord was used as a knot bearer. Since it was hidden within the knots, the knotting appears light.

For the vertical half hitches, the dark cord was used as a knotting cord. Now it hides the light-colored cords and the knotting appears dark.

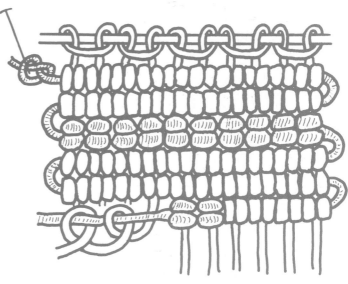

Variations Combining Techniques Shown in Previous Samples

62. Double Half Hitches and Square Knots

63. Decorative "Woven" Diamond

64. Alternating Overhand Knots

65. Strands of Cords Decorated with Overhand Knots

66. Overhand Knots in Two Different Patterns

In the first row, overhand knots are made with groups of three cords. In the second row, overhand knots are made with groups of four cords.

The cords are then split and crossed in the pattern as shown, and in the third row, overhand knots are made with the regrouped sets of four cords.

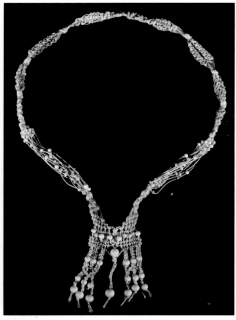

Photo 23. Courtesy *Sylvia Hoffman.*

The Half Hitch and Some Variations

67. Half Hitch Sennit That's Been Allowed to Spiral

A single half hitch was made over and over again around the same core cords. The cord on the right was knotted around the core cords on the left. It spirals of its own accord, but can be coaxed to lie flat.

68. Half Hitch Sennit with Knotting Cords Alternating

Two knotting cords and two central core cords were used. With the knotting cord on the right, a half hitch was made around the core cords. Then, with the knotting cord on the left, a half hitch was made around the core cords. These two steps were repeated throughout.

69. Half Hitch Sennit Variation: Two and Two

Two knotting cords and two central core cords were used. With the knotting cord on the right, two half hitches were made around the core cords. Then, with the knotting cord on the left, two half hitches were made around the core cords. These two steps were repeated throughout.

70. Half Hitch Sennit Variation: Three and Three

Two knotting cords and two central core cords were used. With the knotting cord on the right, three half hitches were made around the core cords. With the knotting cord on the left, three half hitches were made around the core cords. These two steps were repeated throughout.

71. Half Hitch Sennit: Random Pattern

Two knotting cords and two central core cords were used. Knotting cords were hitched around the core cords, first from the right, then from the left in a random pattern.

72. Half Hitch Sennit With Knotting Cords Alternating and Core Cords Split

Two knotting cords and two central core cords were used. With the knotting cord on the right, a half hitch was made around the one core cord adjacent to it. With the same knotting cord, a half hitch was made over the two central core cords. With the knotting cord on the left, a half hitch was made around the one core cord adjacent to it. With the same knotting cord, a half hitch was then made around the two central core cords. These four steps were repeated throughout.

73. Half Hitch Chain or Chain Knot Sennit

Two knotting cords and no core cords were used. With the knotting cord on the right, a half hitch was made around the knotting cord on the left. With the knotting cord on the left, a half hitch was made around the knotting cord on the right. These two steps were repeated throughout.
As each knot is made, it is pushed into place, and tends to rest in a diagonal position.

74. Half Hitch Chain or Chain Knot Sennit, Variation

Four knotting cords and no core cords were used. Two knotting cords were used together as one cord would be used. Then the chain was made as above.

75. Square Knot Sennit with Raised Picot Made of Chain Knots

Four cords were used. A short sennit of square knots was made, using two knotting cords and two core cords. Then, only the two central cords were used, and a short sennit of chain knots was made. The two outside cords were picked up again, and a square knot was made directly below the last square knot. This forced the chain knot sennit to double back on itself and form a raised picot.

Josephine Knots

76. Spaced Josephine Knots

To keep a sennit of Josephine knots from spiraling, reverse the direction of knotting after each Josephine knot is completed.

77. Two-Colored Josephine Knot Band with a Short Sennit of Square Knots

Two light-colored cords and two dark-colored cords were used. The two light-colored cords remained on the outside at all times, while the two dark-colored cords remained on the inside.

Reversed Double Half Hitches and Their Variations

A reversed double half hitch is made in two steps:

Step 1: The knotting cord goes over, around and under the core cord(s), through the loop, and is pushed up into place.

Step 2: The knotting cord goes under, around, and over the core cord(s), through the loop and is pushed up into place.

79. Reversed Double Half Hitch Sennit with the Knots Forming on the Right Side Only

Two cords were used. Reversed double half hitches were made one below the other, using the cord on the right as the knotting cord and the cord on the left as the core cord.

81. Reversed Double Half Hitch Sennit: Two and Two

Using the cord on the right, two reversed double half hitches were made around the two central core cords.

Using the cord on the left, two reversed double half hitches were made around the two central core cords.

These two steps were repeated throughout.

78. Reversed Double Half Hitch Sennit with the Knots Forming on the Left Side Only

Two cords were used. Reversed double half hitches were made one below the other, using the cord on the left as the knotting cord and the cord on the right as the core cord.

80. Reversed Double Half Hitch Sennit with Knots Forming on Both Outside Edges: One and One

Four cords. The two outside cords were used as knotting cords; the two central cords were used as core cords. Using the cord on the right, one reversed double half hitch was made around the two central core cords.

Then using the cord on the left, one reversed double half hitch was made around the two central core cords. This was repeated throughout.

82. Varied Pattern of Reversed Double Half Hitches

83. Six-Strand Reversed Double Half Hitch Pattern Using Only Two Core Cords

The two central cords (4 and 5) were used as the core cords. Using cord 6, one reversed double half hitch was made around the core cords. Then cords 3, 7, 2, 8, and 1 were used in turn to complete on pattern.

84. Two Interlaced Sennits of Reversed Double Half Hitches

Two four-strand sennits of reversed double half hitches are started simultaneously. The sennit on the left is started with the knotting cord on the left which knots around the two core cords; the sennit on the right is started with the knotting cord on the right which knots around two more cords. One reversed double half hitch is made on each sennit. For the second reversed double half hitch, the knotting cord for the right-hand sennit (cord 5) is knotted around the core cords of the left-hand sennit; the knotting cord from the left-hand sennit (cord 4) is knotted around the core cords of the right-hand sennit. These two steps are repeated, with the inside knotting cords interchanging throughout.

85. Two Interlaced Sennits of Reversed Double Half Hitches in a Varied Pattern

Headings

86. Reversed Double Half Hitch with Band in Front

Two different methods of doing this are shown below:

1. The cord to be mounted is folded in half. The center fold is placed on top of, around, and behind the mounting cord or bar. The two free ends are then placed inside the loop and pulled taut.

2. The cord to be mounted is folded in half. The center fold is bent forward and down. The two "ears" that are formed are pushed backwards. The loop that is formed from the folded back "ears" can now be slipped onto a mounting cord or bar and be pulled taut.

87. Reversed Double Half Hitch with Band in Back

Two methods of doing this are shown below:

1. The cord to be mounted is folded in half. The center fold is placed under, around, and in front of the mounting cord or bar. The two free ends are then placed inside the loop and pulled taut.

2. The cord to be mounted is folded in half. The center fold is bent backward and down. The two "ears" that are formed are pulled forward. The loop that is formed with the "ears" can now be slipped onto a mounting cord or bar and be pulled taut.

88. Cords Mounted With Double Half Hitches

The center of a folded cord is slipped under the mounting piece and is pinned to the knotting board close to the mounting piece. A double half hitch is made onto the mounting piece, first with one cord, then with the other.

89. Cords Mounted with Double Half Hitches and a Small Picot

This is made the same as above, except that the folded cord is pinned to the knotting board just a little above the mounting piece.

90. Cords Mounted with Double Half Hitches and a Large Picot

This is the same as the previous one, except that the folded cord is pinned to the knotting board at a still higher point.

91. Cords Mounted with Double Half Hitches and a Double Picot

Two pairs of folded cords are used for this mounting. Both pairs are slipped under the mounting piece and pinned to the knotting board, one above the other. First the two cords on the left are double half hitched onto the mounting piece. Next, the inner picot is completed and then the outer picot is completed.

92. Cords Mounted with Double Half Hitches and a Triple Picot

Three pairs of cords are used for this mounting. All three pairs of cords are slipped under the mount-

ing piece and are pinned to the knotting board, one above the other, as in the diagram. First, the three cords on the left are double half hitched onto the mounting piece. Next, the innermost picot is completed, followed by the middle picot and the outermost picot.

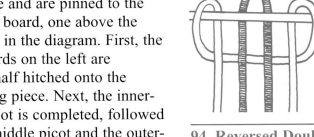

93. Reversed Double Half Hitch Mounting with Inner Cords of One Color and Outer Cords of Another Color. Band in Back

Put the outer cord onto the mounting piece as in number 87, but do not tighten.
Mount the inner cord as in no. 87, slipping these inner cords between the outer cords.
Other methods are possible, but this seems easiest.

94. Reversed Double Half Hitch Mounting with Inner Cords of One Color and Outer Cords of Another Color. Band in Front.

Put the outer cord onto the mounting piece as in number 86, but do not tighten. Mount the inner cord as in no. 86, slipping these inner cords between the outer cords.

95. Two-Color Mounting with Double Half Hitches, a Picot, and a Reversed Double Half Hitch

The outer left cord is hitched onto the mounting piece with a double half hitch as in number 88. The dark middle cords are hitched on with a reversed double half hitch. The outer right cord is then hitched on with a double half hitch.

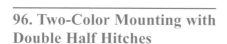

97. Mounting with a Single Overhand Knot and Double Half Hitches

In the center of the mounting cords, an overhand knot is made. The cords are then mounted with double half hitches.

99. Mounting with Double Half Hitches and an Overhand Knot Around the Fold of the Mounting Cords. Small Picot

The mounting cord is folded in half. Holding the two cords together near the fold, an overhand knot is made around the two cords. The cords are then mounted with double half hitches.

96. Two-Color Mounting with Double Half Hitches

The outer left cord is hitched onto the mounting piece with a double half hitch. Then the two central cords are hitched on in the same manner. The outer right cord is hitched on last.

98. Mounting with a Single Overhand Knot, Bead, and Double Half Hitches

An overhand knot is made as above. A bead is then slipped onto the two cords and pushed up until it is just below the overhand knot. The cords are then mounted with double half hitches.

100. Mounting with Double Half Hitches and an Overhand Knot Around the Fold of the Mounting Cords. Large Picot

This is made the same as above except that the overhand knot is further away from the fold in the mounting cord.

101. Mounting with a Bead on Top, an Overhand Knot, and Double Half Hitches

A bead was slipped onto one strand of the mounting cords and was brought up to the center fold. An overhand knot was made just below the bead. The cords were then mounted with double half hitches.

102. Small Single Chain Knot Sennit and Double Half Hitches

A short sennit of two single chain knots was made with two mounting cords. They were then double half hitched onto the mounting piece in the usual manner.

103. Single Chain Knot Sennit and Double Half Hitches

A sennit of four single chain knots was made with two mounting cords. They were then double half hitched onto the mounting piece in the usual manner.

104. Small, Double Chain Knot Sennit and Double Half Hitches

A short sennit of two double chain knots is made with four mounting cords. They are then double half hitched onto the mounting piece in the usual manner.

105. Double Chain Knot Sennit and Double Half Hitches

A sennit of four double chain knots was made with four mounting cords. They were then double half hitched onto the mounting piece in the usual manner.

106. Reversed Double Half Hitched Scalloped Mounting

A pair of mounting cords is hitched onto the mounting piece upside down, with a reversed double half hitch.

Using one of these cords as a knotting cord, and one as a core cord, a sennit of eight reversed double half hitches is made. The sennit is temporarily put aside. Right next to the first pair of mounting cords, three more pairs of mounting cords are hitched onto the mounting piece with reversed double half hitches. The sennit is then arched around toward the mounting piece and the cords double half hitched onto it.

107. Pointed Heading of Square Knots Mounted With Double Half Hitches

One pair of mounting cords is pinned to the knotting board and is opened out to form an upside down

"V" formation. Four pairs of cords are hitched onto either side with reversed double half hitches. Starting from the tip, a pattern of alternating square knots are made until a row of four square knots is completed. All of the cords are then double half hitched onto the mounting piece.

108. Another Method of Making a Pointed Heading (no photo)

109. Single Square Knot Heading with One Picot within Another

One pair of mounting cords is pinned to the knotting board; these cords are core cords. A second pair is pinned to the board a little above the first; these are the knotting cords. With the knotting cords, one square knot is made around the core cords. The cords are then double half hitched onto the mounting piece in the usual manner

110. Square Knot Heading with One Picot within Another

This is made the same as that above, except that two square knots are made around the core cords.

111. Single Square Knot Heading with One Picot Beside the Other

Two pairs of mounting cords are pinned to the knotting board, one beside the other. The two center cords are the core cords, the two outside cords are the knot-ting cords. With the knotting cords, one square knot is made around the core cords. The cords are then hitched on to the mounting piece with double half hitches in the usual manner.

112. Square Knot heading with One Picot Beside the Other

This is made the same as the sample above, except that two square knots are made around the core cords.

113. Square Knot Heading with Three Picots, One Beside the Other

Three pairs of mounting cords are pinned to the knotting board, one beside the other. The center pair should be higher than the outside pairs. The two outside cords are the knotting cords; the four inner cords are the core cords. With the two outside knotting cords, one square knot is made around the four core cords. The cords are then double half hitched onto the mounting piece in the usual manner.

Circular Pieces

It is best to work a circular piece on a knotting board that can be rotated easily. Knotting cords can be mounted on anything that is round - either a solid ring, or a ring made of cord. Cords can be hitched onto the ring with reversed double half hitches, double half hitches, and sometimes even in a more fanciful manner.

Circles are usually worked from the center out, since it's more convenient to add cords than to drop them. Any combination of knots can be used but as the circle grows, more cords are generally needed. There are many different ways in which cords can be added. The samples illustrate some ways of adding cords.

114. Circular Piece: One

For the mounting ring, a cord was cut, and shaped into a ring with the ends overlapping. Ten pairs of knotting cords were mounted onto this ring with reversed double half hitches. Sennits of alternating square knots with an open net-like effect were made as in number 25. New cords were added onto the "floats" between the alternating square knots. Pairs of cords were hitched onto each "float" with a reversed double half hitch. They were then knotted into sennits of square knots.

115: Circular Piece: Two

For the mounting ring, a small curtain ring was used. Cords were mounted onto the ring with reversed double half hitches. A small pattern of alternating square knots was made.

A new knot-bearing cord was pinned to the knotting board. The cords from one group of square knots were double half hitched onto the new knot bearer. Then two pairs of new knotting cords were hitched onto the knot bearer with reversed double half hitches. The last two steps were repeated all around the circle. A second row of double half hitches was made and the knotting pattern continued.

Adding Cords

116. Adding or Increasing the Number of Cords

In this sample, one way of adding cords is shown. The sample was started with four pairs of cords hitched onto a dowel with reversed double half hitches. Two sennits of square knots were made and the cord was then double half hitched onto a second dowel. At this point, more cords were desired. Between the two sennits, two additional pairs of cords were mounted with double half hitches and a double picot as in number 91. The pair of cords on either side of the sennits were double half hitched on with a single picot as in no. 90. The two outermost cords were hitched on with a reversed double half hitch with the band in the back as in no. 87.

There are many other ways of adding cords. Two of these ways are shown on the circular samples.

Actually, any place that will hold a new cord securely is fair game.

Cords don't necessarily need to be mounted straight down. They can be mounted on a slant, or sideways, and the knotting can continue in a new direction.

Shaping Pieces

117. Shaping Pieces Sample

This sample illustrates two different methods of shaping a piece of macramé. The right side of the sample has a gradual outward curve. In a pattern of alternating square knots, such as in this sample, vertical floats form along the edges. To achieve the gradual curve, one pair of new cords was hitched onto each vertical float. The new cords were immediately incorporated into the knotting pattern. The left side of the sample has a rather abrupt outward curve. A new pair of cords was hitched onto a float at the edge of the sample. The new cords curved over to the left - and became new mounting cords. Additional cords were mounted onto them, and the alternating square knot pattern was continued.

These methods of shaping are particularly well suited to shaping articles of clothing. As a guide for your knotting, you can draw your pattern onto a piece of paper and pin the paper to your knotting board, or you can buy a commercial pattern and pin it to your knotting board.

And these are some of the variations possible with just a few knots - and a little imagination.

Chapter Three

Photo 24. Top view of Pandora's Box. Vertical and horizontal half hitches. *Susan Gable Williamson*.

How Long Is Long Enough?

How long is long enough? What if you run out of a cord? What are some ways of shortening cords temporarily? And what other materials and equipment work well with macramé? These are some very practical problems that need some very practical solutions.

Equipment

The equipment needed to get started in macramé is delightfully simply. The only essentials are a knotting board, scissors, pins, and the yarns you will use. A few very helpful accessories are rubber bands, a crochet hook, a large-holed tapestry needle, a measuring device, and graph paper or paper with a grid of squares and angles.

Knotting Boards

Most projects in macramé will be worked on a flat work surface, or knotting board. To make knotting easier, strong pins will be pushed into the knotting board. You will pull against these pins while making and tightening the knots. Therefore, a sturdy surface and one that will accept pins is needed.

The two materials mentioned earlier and most satisfactory for this purpose are:

1. A polyurethane or plastic foam kneeling pad or pillow form. *Plastic foam* - not foam rubber. A convenient size is 12" x 16". The kneeling pad can be purchased

in hardware and variety stores; the pillow form in fabric or upholstery stores.

2. Insulating board about 12" x 16". Insulating board is generally available in lumberyards where, occasionally, scraps can be found. Often a whole sheet (48" x 96") or a half sheet (48" x 48") must be purchased. However, a whole sheet is relatively inexpensive. The cost would be reduced, of course, if you could share the sheet with some other people. Some craft suppliers carry this type of board, too. Some brands of insulating board are more satisfactory than others. If the pin penetrates the material without your having to apply too much pressure and if you can pull against the pin without displacing it, the board should work well for macramé.

If you cannot obtain a foam kneeling pad or a small piece of insulating board, you can make a knotting board for yourself out of the following materials. They will be somewhat less satisfactory than a polyurethane pad or an insulating board, but they will work adequately.

3. Several thicknesses of corrugated cardboard taped or glued together at the edges. The sides of empty boxes you find at the supermarket are ideal for this purpose. A convenient size is 12" x 16", but it doesn't matter if it is a little larger or smaller. Put enough thicknesses of cardboard together to make the board about one inch thick.

4. A very firmly stuffed pillow. It must be stuffed firmly enough so that the stuffing will not move as you are working on the pillow.

5. A few thicknesses of cork or foamcore glued at the edges or taped together. A board made with these should be at least 3/4 of an inch thick. To reduce the cost, a few layers may be glued to corrugated cardboard to get it up to the necessary thickness. Use glue around the edges only.

Or, make your own as of old:

"Make the cushion as an oblong flat-shaped pillow, 12" long by 8" wide, and stuff it with sand to render it heavy, cover it with good Ticking [sic] and arrange the lines woven in the Ticking evenly along the length of the cushion, as they can then be used as guides for the horizontal lines of the work. An ornamental cover of scarlet ingrain twill, or blue silk can be arranged over the ticking cover, if the latter is not considered ornamental enough, but it is not necessary. Prepare a piece of fine linen or silk, similar in shape to the Covers used in other Pillow Lace making to pin over the lace while in progress to keep it clean."
(from S.F.A. Caulfield and Blanch C. Saward, *Dictionary of Needlework*, 1885.)

Photo 25. Basic Materials and Tools for Macramé.

Knotting or Mounting Surfaces for Various Special Uses

While working on a belt or other small piece, a clipboard lined with a piece of polyurethane foam is convenient. The top of the knotting can be fastened under the clip and the knotter can pull against this. It is a good traveling companion.

For large pieces, or when macramé comes to fill your heart and home, you might find the following helpful.

A draftsman's drawing table is ideally suited for macramé. You can raise, lower, and tilt it to any angle which is most comfortable for you for any given project. Cover the top of the table with insulating board.

My upright tapestry loom now has a piece of insulating board clamped to its front surface. (A sturdy easel would be its equivalent.) This provides a permanent work area and a comfortable one. You can sit or stand before this and work. When you stop working, the knotting can stay pinned to this surface. Tangling of cords is minimized in this way.

Three-dimensional hanging pieces present their own problems. Suspending the piece from a hook in a doorway works well - except that lighting and traffic are often problems.

Here is another solution that's more convenient in several ways. It allows you to work wherever you please, sitting or standing. The piece you are working on may be raised or lowered to meet your needs. All that is involved is a screw eye mounted in the ceiling near where you work, and two specially prepared cords.

Photo 26. Work in progress. *Jennifer Bress.*

To Make a Hanger for Working on Three-Dimensional Pieces

Screw a large screw eye into the ceiling. Cut a strong cord two yards long. You may need a longer cord if your ceiling is higher than eight feet.

Slip a swivel hook onto the cord. (A swivel hook is the type used for dog leashes.)

Slip one end of the cord through the screw eye in the ceiling.

Join the two ends of the cord with an overhand knot.

Cut another cord two yards long.

Put it through the top of your macramé piece and tie the two ends together.

Make overhand knots along this cord about every two inches.

Hook this cord onto the swivel hook at whatever height is comfortable for you. You may sit or stand as your work. When your hanging needs to be raised, unhook it, and move it up a notch or two. For a wide hanging, two sets of hangers will work well.

Shaped Pieces

Since cords can be added to or eliminated from a piece of macramé, macramé pieces can be made in almost any shape you please. Clothing, for example, can be made by knotting directly over a paper pattern. Using forms as a base, on the other hand, allows you to construct three-dimensional pieces. Martha Hoering worked the bell in photo 27 around a cone of yarn. Pins penetrate the yarn easily. Styrofoam forms, dress forms, and wig stands are just a few of the things you can use as a base on which to construct three-dimensional pieces. When a slick surface must be used, the knots can be urged to stay in place temporarily with double-stick cellophane tape or masking tape.

Photo 28. Macramé Vest. *Joan Michaels Paque*. Photo, *Hank Paque*.

Photo 27. Bell. How did she do it? For a knotting base, Martha Hoering used a cone of yarn. She pinned the center of a heavy cord to this cone. Onto the heavy cord, she hitched some fine cotton yarn. The heavy cords meander around and the fine cotton cord is double half-hitched onto it. *Martha Hoering.*

Photo 29. Shaped Collar. *Mary Belle Frey.*

Other Miscellaneous Equipment

Scissors: Any pair sturdy enough to cut the cords you choose.

Pins: Sturdy pins are important. "T" pins, sometimes called "Wig" pins are most satisfactory for use with insulating board. They can be found in craft shops, sewing supply stores, or where hair accessories, such as bobby pins, are sold. It's well to have about two dozen on hand. "U" pins, sometimes called "Tidy" pins work beautifully with the plastic foam. They are usually sold where sewing or upholstery supplies are sold.

Rubber Bands: One method of shortening the working cords you use is to "bundle" up each long cord and hold each "bundle" with a rubber band. If you choose this method, you'll need as many rubber bands as there are cords in your project. This and other ways to shorten cords are shown on page 66.

Knitting Bobbins: Sometimes large knitting bobbins can be used to shorten cords. They are available in knitting stores and come with directions for use.

Crochet hook and large tapestry needle: These are used primarily to end cords off when finishing a project.

Measuring tools: For small projects, a yardstick is very satisfactory for measuring the length of cords you need. When you begin to work on larger pieces, other means are more satisfactory. Two chairs set at an appropriate distance apart will serve well. I think, however, that a weaver's warping board is most satisfactory for measuring long cords. One may be purchased at a weaver's supply house or reproduced simply at home. Methods for using these devices will be described later.

Making a Measuring Board

You will need the following materials which are readily available in any lumber yard:

One pine board: ask for size 1" x 12" x 42". The actual measurements of the board they will give you will be 3/4" x 11 1/2" x 42".

Eight 3" finishing nails. Get a few extra ones in case they bend as you hammer them in.

Put in nails as indicated on the diagram.

With this measuring board, you can measure cords as short as 18 inches and as long as 12 yards. The board is small enough to be put away in a closet when not in use.

Accessories For Use With Macramé

To add to the fun and excitement of macramé, start the happy search for beads, buckles, bells, seeds, feathers, shells, and anything you feel might add interest to a piece of knotting.

Photo 30. Necklace. In this neckpiece, the peacock contributed in a very personal way. Courtesy *Thurid Clark. Karen Wise.*

Beads: All kinds of beads are available, but knotters have a special problem. Often macramé is worked with heavy yarns, and often more than one strand of yarn must pass through the hole of a bead. Therefore, beads with large holes are generally needed. With care, the holes in some beads can be enlarged. For example, the holes in wood or cork beads can be enlarged either by drilling them out or by poking a heated rod through their centers.

Enlarging Holes In Wooden or Cork Beads

Drilling: Hold the bead firmly in a vise or with a pair of pliers, then drill with a hand or electric drill.
Burning out the center: Have ready some asbestos or some other fireproof and heat-resistant material such as a ceramic tile or brick, and an ice pick or a steel rod about 12 inches long and about 1/8 inch in diameter. The rod can be purchased in hobby stores where they are generally sold for use as the landing gears of model airplanes.

Place the bead in a vise or hold it with a pair of pliers. Heat the rod in the flame of your stove. When the tip of the rod is red hot, using your pliers, pick the rod up at the opposite end and push it through the center of the bead.

While the rod is still hot, try burning lines and dots on the bead itself and turn an otherwise ordinary bead into a rather unique one.
Filing: The holes in some beads might be enlarged by filing them with a jeweler's files. Many hardware stores, as well as some of the better stocked craft and hobby stores, carry jeweler's files.

Photo 31. Earrings. *Madge Schneider.*

Now For The Hunt

Somewhere within your home, you probably have the beginning of a bead collection: a broken necklace or a worn-out beaded purse. A variety store can hold some treasures: try the jewelry counter and the toy sections. Import houses may have strings of glass beads as well as beads made from seeds or wood. For a very special piece, you might select beads from a jeweler, a lapidary shop, or a museum shop. Don't forget the craft shops and bead stores, too!

Handmade beads and macramé combine particularly well. Some potters make and sell them themselves or sell them through craft or bead shops. You can make beads yourself. Clay, polymer clay, papier-mâché, instant papier-mâché, large seed pods, scraps of wood, sea shells, and square and round tubing available from hobby stores, are just some of the raw materials you can start with.

Photo 32. Sash with Handmade Ceramic Beads. *Hannelies Penner.*

The search for buckles and rings of various sizes may lead you to fabric shops, notions counters, hardware stores, and marine supply houses; for decorative buckles to leather supply shops, museum shops, shops that sell American Indian handicrafts, as well as to antique shops.

For bells you might try import houses, craft stores, and gift shops.

For seeds (not to be confused with "seed beads" which are tiny beads that are impractical for use with macramé) look in import houses or variety stores. They often have strings of beads made from seeds.

Try craft shops for feathers. If you're adventurous and not too squeamish, you can sometimes find freshly killed birds on country roads. One bird has a lot of feathers.

It's fun to use shells you've collected yourself, but that's not always possible. Craft shops, tropical fish stores, and shell specialty stores are good sources for these.

A macramé piece may be mounted on holding cords or it may be started on almost anything that strikes your fancy. Here are some mounting pieces to consider: dowels, sticks, plastic rods, bamboo, parts of old chairs, purse handles, buckles, ceramic pieces, curtain rods, and knitting needles.

More ideas will be discussed in the chapter on design.

Measurements

How long is long enough? Usually, it's longer than you think! For several good reasons, teachers and writers wish you wouldn't ask that embarrassing question. Unless a project has been knotted before, and is going to be repeated exactly, there is no one, direct, specific answer.

This leaves the teacher or writer in a rather uncomfortable spot. He may guess just right - and all is well. If he overestimates, you will have yarn left over - and he will be blamed for wasting your material. If he underestimates - well, that really is a nuisance!

Here is the basic problem.

In order to determine exactly how much yarn you need for a particular project, you need to know the amount of take-up (amount of yarn consumed in making a knot) plus how many knots and which kinds you will be placing on each cord. Only rarely will you have all this information in advance and so I offer the following suggestions.

If you don't have a plan in mind, just want to create a piece as you go along, and don't know how open or close the knotting will be, you can take a chance and estimate with this rule of thumb:

The length of each cord should be about four times the length of the finished piece.

However, if the cords are to be folded in half, the length of each cord should be 8 times the length of the finished piece, but only half as many cords will be needed.

This rule of thumb usually works well for those pieces that have some open and some closed areas.

For example, let us say that you are planning a narrow hanging about one yard long. You plan to use 24 cords mounted on a dowel. You would measure, then, only 12 cords, each eight yards long. When folded on a dowel, that will give you the 24 cords you need, and each cord will be four yards long.

The chart on page 69 lists a large variety of cords. To determine the approximate number of cords per inch of a fairly dense piece, take a ruler and wrap your cord around it for an inch with the cords touching lightly. Count and multiply by the total width desired.

To determine the total amount of yardage needed for a given piece, multiply:

the length of each cord x **the number of cords = the total amount of yardage required for the piece**

There are many good reasons for making a sample before you start on a particular project. A sample gives you the opportunity to experiment with different knot-

Photo 33. Test Samples. May Shields finds this visual record very helpful. *May Shields.* Photo, *Seymour Bress.*

ting patterns and gives you time to get the "feel" of the yarn. After experimenting with the type of pattern you plan to use, you can then measure your finished sample, and be able to approximate the amount of yarn you'll need for your actual piece.

Here's a suggestion on how to make a sample:

Cut four cords, each cord six feet (or two yards) long. Fold each cord in half and mount each cord on a cord or on a small dowel. Experiment with the cords, try different knots and several different patterns. When most of the yarn is used up, measure your finished sample.

The formula for determining the length of cords you will need for your project, based on a sample is:

                    divided
length of starting cords ÷ length of finished sample of your sample   **by**

                                  = your base number

The base number multiplied by the length of your planned piece will give you the length of each cord you will need for your project. Remember, though, if the cords will be folded in half, double the length and cut only half as many cords.

Your base number x **length of your planned piece = length of each cord. (Double this if the cords are to be folded in half.)**

Whether or not your cords are to be folded in half, add a few inches for a fringe and for working space. Very short ends are hard to work with.

With experience, you'll learn that some knots consume more yarn than others. Then, you'll either compensate for this in figuring the amount of yarn you'll need, or you'll learn to splice very well.

It goes without saying that a dense knotting pattern needs longer cords than an open one. The knotting cord in vertical half hitches gets used up at a phenomenal rate. Core cords of sennits, on the other hand, have practically no take-up at all.

How To Measure

When measuring yarns with a yardstick, wrap the yarn around and around the yardstick the long way until the proper length is reached. Cut and use this first cord as a measuring guide for the others. Cut the remaining cords using the first cord as a guide and place each cord in a separate pile. This keeps the cords from tangling.

Two Chair Method of Measuring

The two-chair method works like this. Place two chairs half as far apart as the total length of the cords needed. Tie one end of the cord to chair 1. Bring the cord around chair 2 and back to chair 1. One cord has now been measured.

Continue in this way. When the total number of cords has been measured, cut the cords at Chair 1 only. The halfway mark is around Chair 2.

Measuring Board

I feel that the measuring board described on page 62 is the most satisfactory device of all for measuring macramé cords. Place the board on a table. Make a loop near the end of your string and secure it with an overhand knot. Place the loop around the nail (A). To measure off an eight-yard cord, take the cord and bring it around nail (B); bring the cord back around nail (C); bring the cord over to the right again and around nail (D) and then back again, but this time around nail (E). You have now measured off four yards.

To measure off the other half of this cord, follow the same path you just took - but in reverse. The first cord will serve as a guide. When you get back to nail (A) you have measured off one eight-yard cord. Repeat these steps for all the cords of this length you need.

Tie the cords at nail E and cut the cords at the starting nail (nail A) only. Nail (E) is your halfway mark. Cords can be removed one at a time. If you remove them at nail (E), they are already folded in half and can be mounted onto your mounting piece directly.

Mounting Cords

After measuring off your cords, the next logical step is to mount them. This may be done in several ways. They may be pinned to a board or hitched onto a bar as shown on pages 49-54.

Average Sizes

Belts: Waist measure plus a few inches for overlap.
Sashes: Waist measure plus about 20" fringe on either side. (To estimate the yardage needed for each strand of a sash: take waist measure, multiply it by 4, and add about 40" for the fringe.
Leash: 5 feet.
Pillows
       square: 12" x 12" or 14" x 14"
       round: 12" or 14" diameter
       floor: 24" square
Place Mats: 12" x 18" or 14" x 21"
Purses
       Handbag: 8" x 10"
       Evening: 4 1/2" x 7 1/2"
       Small Tote: 10" x 10" plus fringe
       Large Tote: 14" x 14" plus fringe
Runners: 14" x 28"
Stoles: 17" x 60" plus a fringe on each end
       22" x 90" plus a fringe on each end

Shortening Cords

Most often your cords will be very long and knotting would become tedious if the cords were not shortened. There are several satisfactory ways of shortening cords.

1. Starting from a point about 18 inches below your mounting piece, wind the cord around your palm. Keep wrapping the yarn round and round your palm, always placing the cord alongside the previous cord and working out toward your fingertips. When you have completely wound the cord, slip it off your hand and place a rubber band around the center. If the winding was done carefully, the cord will release easily as the knotting progresses. If done carelessly you'll have to undo it occasionally, and rewrap.

2. A variation of this is known to weavers and other craftsmen as a "butterfly." Again, start from a point about 18 inches below the mounting piece.

Begin by putting the cord between your thumb and index finger of your right hand.

Bring the cord across your palm and bring it around your little finger.

Next, bring the cord around the outside of your thumb and then between your thumb and index finger. Continue in this way back and forth.

Try not to overlap the cord as you bring it around your fingers. Keep the cord moving up toward the tips of your fingers.

Stop winding when you have a few inches of cord left. With your left hand, firmly hold the center of the "bobbin" you've formed.

Remove the bobbin from your fingers.

Wrap the free end of the cord tightly around the middle of the bobbin several times.

Tie the loose end of the cord with one or two hitches. What you've actually made is a small pull skein. The cord should release easily and continually. The description is wordy, but the butterfly is easy to make and pleasant to use.

3. If neither of these two shortening methods appeal to you, you might like to use knitting bobbins. Sometimes extra large ones are available in yarn shops. Directions for use should come with them. You'll need one bobbin for each cord you have.

"Butterfly"

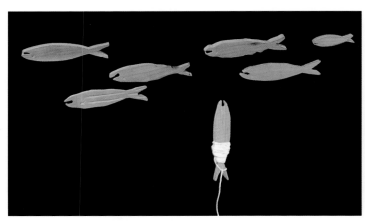

Photo 34. Fish. In earlier times fish bobbins of this sort were used. *Steve Bress*

Splicing

Sometimes it happens! You run out of cord, or a cord breaks. All is not lost. There are several relatively easy ways of remedying this situation.

Usually you are aware that a cord is shortening and that you'll soon need to replace it. In such a case, you can often arrange to replace it at your convenience and in a convenient spot. Here are the most convenient spots:

1. When making sennits of square knots, or half square knots, the core cords are easily replaceable. Any core cord can be replaced this way.

2. When you are making a sennit as below and a knotting cord begins to shorten too quickly, you can interchange the knotting cord with one of the core cords and continue knotting. If you are a perfectionist, you may not like this method, because upon close scrutiny the change is slightly noticeable.

3. When making double half hitches, the knot-bearing cord is simple to replace. Overlap the old knot-bearing cord with the new one, and do several double half hitches over both ends together. Clip off the old cord, and continue with the new one. If the knot-bearing cord is very thick, you might like to cut out a ply or two of both the old and the new cords, and then overlap them.

Although the splicing techniques described above are the easiest to manage, other situations can be remedied too.

4. Sometimes an old and a new cord can be knotted together on the wrong side of the piece, and the macramé portion can go right on. This method of splicing will only work when the knotting is dense enough to hide the joining knot. The knot-bearing cord in vertical half hitches can usually be replaced in this way.

5. Another method is to drop the short cord before it gets shorter than four inches. Pin a new cord to your board, leaving a tail of about four or five inches. Continue knotting, using the replacement cord. When the piece is completed, return to the spot where you added the new cord and either weave the old and new ends back into some knots to keep the cords from coming loose, or knot the two ends together, or stitch the ends down inconspicuously, or, if necessary, glue the ends down. If the piece will not be washed, any white glue will do. If it will be washed, it's best to use a waterproof fabric glue.

And now for the traditional way of splicing two cords together.

6. In this method of splicing, the old cord is joined directly to a new cord. Most yarns used for macramé are composed of several strands - or plies - twisted together.

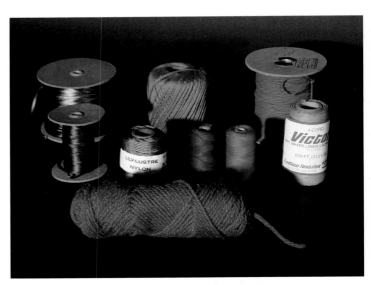

Photo 36. An assortment of yarns including rattail, soutache, crochet cotton, and rug yarn.

Untwist the new and the old cord for a distance of about two inches. Overlap the plies from both cords (see diagram). Twist a ply from one cord together with a ply from the other. (If possible, twist them in the direction opposite to the way they were originally twisted. They seem to hold together better this way.) Twist the rest of the plies together in the same way. When all the plies are twisted together, the knotting can be continued. If the splice is not too secure, a thin solution of glue can be used to hold it in place. Also, if the splice is too thick, one or more sets of plies can be cut out.

Appropriate Materials

Generally, knotters look for a strong, smooth, hard-twisted, non-elastic cord. This combination of qualities works well for macramé. With experience - and care - other combinations can be used to good advantage.

Photo 37. Seine twine, sisal, jute, and upholstery twine.

Photo 35. Waxed linen comes in many attractive colors. Yarns courtesy of Helby Import Co., Linden, New Jersey.

Seine Twine

Polypropylene Cord

Jute, 3 Ply

Seine Twine #36

Jute 2 Ply

Rayon Satin or Rattail #2

Tubular Cotton

Rug Yarn (Rayon and Cotton)

Rug Yarn (Wool)

Knitting Worsted (Wool)

Knitted Worsted (Orlon)

Seine Twine #21 (Nylon)

Seine Twine #21 (Cotton)

Rayon Satin or Rattail #1

Photo 38.

Soutache

Seine Twine #18 (Nylon)

Seine Twine #18 (Cotton)

Sisal

Waxed Linen

Macramé Cord

Polished Indian Twine

10/5 Linen

Navy Cord

Heavy Crochet Thread

Spring Twine - Heavy Weight

Tarred Marline

Mattress Twine

Upholstery or Mattress Twine

Perle Cotton 3/2

Photo 39.

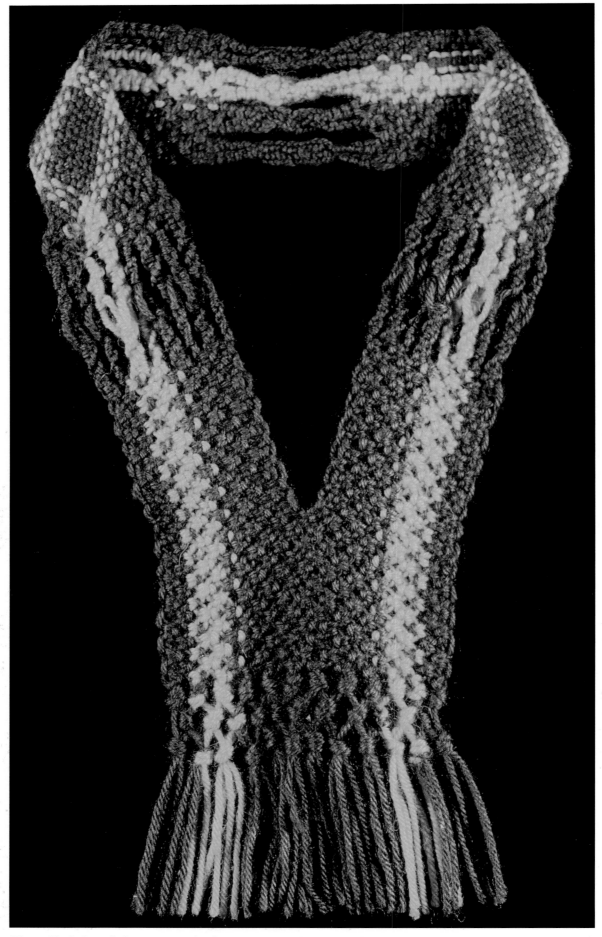

Chapter Four

Photo 40. Soft neckpiece, made of soft yarns, square knots, and finger weaving at the shoulder part. It's ended with a few rows of overhand knots. *Marjorie Newell.*

Beginnings and Endings
& some in-betweens

Endings

I ncongruous as it may seem, let's start with some endings. Although, different types of projects have problems unique unto themselves, they all come to an end and often, the same type of ending can be used for diverse projects. Care should be taken in choosing an appropriate ending so that the lines or contours of the endings follow or are in keeping with the feel of the rest of the piece. A delicate, prim wall hanging, for example, could be spoiled by ending it with fat clumps of overhand knots and an untrimmed fringe.

Fringes and macramé are a natural. A fringe may be secured with overhand knots, wrapping, or double half hitches. A fringe may be trimmed evenly all across or deliberately unevenly - but with thought, please. Yes, sloppiness may make something unique, but it doesn't often produce good design.

The strip sample on page 116 illustrates several different ways of ending a piece. Other examples can be found throughout the book.

The overhand knot method is one of the most common ways

of ending a piece. The neckpiece in Photo 40 and the sash in Photo 42 are two examples of this.

Photo 42. Sash. This tri-colored sash is ended with a row of overhand knots. *Ella Bolster.*

Photo 41. Detail of Photo 236. *Ruth Gainer.*

Wrapping

Wrapping produces a less bulky, neat fringe. The ending cords may be wrapped with a color the same as the fringe, or with colors to match other parts of the hanging. The detail on the right is a good example of this.

Photo 43. Detail of Macramé Hanging. *Helene Bress.*

If the cord isn't too wiry or springy, a row of double half hitches can end the piece and a fringe left below it. The row of double half hitches can be straight or shaped. The bottom rear of the hanging on page 126 is shaped with double half hitches and trimmed. If the cord is springy, a row of overhand knots below the double half hitches will usually keep the cords in place.

Tassels

Tassels can be an effective "ending" for window shade pulls or at corners of pillows. One way to make a tassel is like this:

For the core of your tassel

Measure off a batch of cords twice the length of your tassel-to-be. (You can do this easily around a piece of stiff cardboard cut to the length of your tassel.)

For the decorative portion of your tassel

Measure off some more cords about six times the length of your tassel. These

Photo 44. Tassels. *Mary Belle Frey.*

cords may be the same color or a contrasting color. More cords can be added or some removed, if necessary. Have the number of cords be a multiple of four, e.g., 16, 20, 24.

Place the longer cords on top of the core cords.

Cut two more cords for the "hanger" part of your tassel.

Place the "hanger" cords around the center of all the tassel cords. Draw the cords together tightly and make a knot.

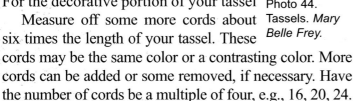

Pin the "hanger" cords to your knotting board and add some decorative knotting with your long tassel cords.

Knot the "hanger" cords into a decorative sennit.

Trim all ends.

Stand back and admire!

Photo 45. Tassels. Linen tassels for shade pulls. *Mary Belle Frey.*

Other Methods

There are many instances when fringes and tassels are not desirable. Here are a few ways you can end a piece without either.

1. Turn the piece to the wrong side. With a large-eyed tapestry needle or crochet hook, bring the ends up and through a few knots in the previous rows. If the piece will not get any abuse and the cord is not springy, the cord can then be trimmed. If the piece will be handled a bit, after the cord is tucked back into a few knots, make an overhand knot in the cord, leave a little tail, and trim.

2. Another method of getting the cords to the wrong side of the piece is to make a final row of reversed double half hitches. The cords are now on the back of your piece, and may be tucked back into a few knots as above, or treated as those which follow.

3. Ends can be brought to the back and stitched down by hand.

4. Ends can be brought to the back and glued down with white glue or special fabric glue. If the piece is washable, be sure the glue is also washable. Fabric glues are usually washable; white glues are usually not.

5. Clothing, pillows, and purses will often be faced or lined. Ends should be treated as above and then the piece should be faced or lined in the usual manner.

Ending of Endings

A little ingenuity will go a long way. When all else fails, improvise. You're bound to come up with a good solution.

Beginnings

The choices for mounting or starting pieces are infinite. They run the gamut from a piece of string to precious gems. As you browse through this book, you'll see many interesting mounting pieces, and in Chapter 5 there are some ideas which may intrigue you. Plain headings and more fanciful ones are described on pages 49-54. While you may start your project on almost anything that suits your fancy, you may have to improvise some way to mount your cords. A piece of driftwood will serve as a good example.
Here's some driftwood.

You may want to:
1. Mount the cords directly around the piece as in "a"
2. Drill some holes in it and mount the cords as in "b"
3. Drill a few holes in the driftwood and suspend a bar from it as in "c"

Each way will give you a different effect - but all three ways will work.

Sometimes, you want to get started right now, but you're not quite sure what you want to start on. Within limits, you can transfer your work from one bar to another after the work has begun. Transferring your work from bars of equal size (e.g., from a 1/2 inch dowel to a 1/2 inch plastic rod) is relatively easy. Just butt the two ends together and gently slip the piece off one bar directly onto the other.

The same method holds for transferring your work from a larger rod to a smaller one. In that case, there will be a small area of strings showing before the knotting part begins.

You can even transfer your work to a considerably larger starting piece. To make such a transfer, remove your macramé piece from its original mounting bar. The original mounting hitches will open to about twice their original size. The rest of the knotting will not become undone. You can then slip your piece back onto any suitable mounting piece.

Belts and Sashes

Belts have their own set of requirements.

"D" rings and "O" rings are versatile and well suited for macramé belts. Wooden, metal, and strong plastic rings are sometimes available in sewing supply shops; metal rings can be found in hardware stores, marine supply stores, and in craft shops which sell leather-working supplies and equipment. Two "O" or "D" rings mounted together form a good buckle. One of the first projects in the book is made this way. (See page 11).

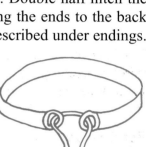

Another way to use these rings is to mount the starting cords on one ring with double half hitches, make the belt a few inches shorter than your waist measurement, and mount the other ring at the end. Double half hitch the cords onto the second ring, bring the ends to the back and finish in one of the ways described under endings.

To hold the belt together, make a tie cord about 18 inches long. Slip this through both rings and tie it in the middle. Small curtain rings or inexpensive finger rings can also be used for these belts.

Any buckle may be used for a belt. You can mount the cords directly onto the buckle or start the belt at the tip.

1. Mount the cords directly onto the buckle. Knot your belt long enough to completely circle your waist, plus an additional few inches for overlap. In the pattern on the overlap, provide secure places into which the "tongue" of the buckle can fit securely, such as alternating square knots.

2. Start the belt at the tip, perhaps with a point as described in the knot variations section. Continue knotting until the belt completely circles your waist plus a few additional inches for an overlap. Divide your cords, and

Photo 46. Belt. Eight heavy rayon cords were mounted onto two large rings. A simple pattern of alternating square knots was used to make this handsome belt. *Melissa Diamanti.*

make a few sennits of square knots about 1 1/2 inches long. Fold the sennits around the buckle and secure them by sewing them down on the back of the belt. End off the cords.

A belt may also be started with a loop and held together with a large knot, button, bead, or bar at the other end as the necklace on page 77.

A leather belt may be trimmed with macramé as in "a".

This can be done by making several sets of holes about six inches apart down the length of the belt. To come out properly, there must be an even number of sets of holes, i.e., 4, 6, 8. Mount your cords through the first set of holes at one end of the belt, and start knotting. When the knotting reaches the second set of holes, push the ends through those holes, bring the cords up through the next set of holes and begin knotting again. At the last set of holes, push your cords through to the back of the belt and make some square knots to secure the macramé, or glue the cords to the leather.

Perhaps you have a leather belt which is no longer being used. You can cut off a few inches from the beginning of the belt and a few inches of the tip of the belt. Push or punch a few holes in each piece, as in "b". Mount your macramé cords through these holes and knot until the belt you are knotting and the tip which was cut off the leather belt go around your waist properly. Push the ends through the tip end of the leather belt and end them as in one of the "endings."

If you did the above belt, you now have a strip of leather left over - the center of the belt you just cut up. How about pushing or punching some holes on either end of this piece of leather, as in "c"? Mount cords in the holes and do some fancy knotting. Tie it around your waist as a sash. Note: Be sure that the leather portion is smaller than your waist so that the sash will tie around the knotting and drape well.

Photo 47. (left) Belt. Belt of white nylon seine twine. Note the ingenious way in which spaces were created so that the belt could be secured. *Margaret Overholt.*

Photo 48. (right) Belt with Buckle. This interesting pattern of double half hitches was knotted with a smooth shiny rayon cord (rattail). *Doramay Keasbey.*

A sash may be knotted in the same general pattern from end to end, or knotted rather solidly around the waist portion, and ended with long fringes - plain or elaborate. The overlap for a sash is usually about 20 inches for each side, 40 inches total.

Photo 50. (above) Sash. Natural linen sash with variegated green beads. The fringes are made of chain knot sennits which are wrapped at the ends to hold them securely. *Helene Bress.*

Photo 51 (right) Sash. Marie Grassi ended her colorful sash by wrapping the cords at the waist and then letting the cords cascade down. *Marie Grassi.*

Photo 49. Sash. Trudy Nicholson freely improvised the knotting on this elaborate sash. Gold, heavyweight, crochet cotton. *Trudy Nicholson.*

Photo 52. Three Belts. Here are some ideas for the "in-between" portion of your belt or sash. *Trudy Nicholson, Ella Bolster, Helene Bress.*

Necklaces

Where to start? How to end?
Possibilities are numerous. Probably the simplest of all is to start with a string, mount cords directly onto it, and tie the mounting string with a bow in the back.

You can start a necklace with a loop at one end and end it with a bead, button, or bar which will fit through the loop and close the necklace. A bead works well if the loop and bead are matched well, but I think the button or bar is a bit more secure.

To start a necklace in this way:
1. Take two of your cords, and fold them in half.
2. Tie an overhand knot just below the fold.
3. Leave enough of a loop to accommodate your bead, button, or bar.

To end with a bead:
1. Take one or more cords and pull them through the bead from the right.
2. Then take an equal number of cords and pull them through the bead again, but this time from the left.
3. Now take these cords, and make a square knot below the bead.
4. Work the ends back into the piece.

It's often easier to find a button that fits the starting loop than to try to match up a loop and a bead. If you're going to use a button to close your necklace, finish the knotting portion by stitching or gluing the ends down, or by bringing the ends back in, as described previously in "Endings," page 72.
Find a button that fits the loop securely and sew it onto the end.

To end with a hook and eye or Velcro:
A sturdy hook and eye or Velcro will work well, too. These can be sewn directly onto the finished piece.

Photo 53. Neckpiece. Trudy Nicholson started this piece on the ceramic disk in the center - and worked her way down. She then decided it would make a nice neckpiece, turned the piece upside down - and completed the neck part. *Trudy Nicholson.*

Photo 54. Chose-up of Neckpiece. This neckpiece closes with a loop and a bar. Trudy Nicholson used a piece of hollow tubing for the bar, ran her cords through it, wrapped the bar, and secured the ends with glue. *Trudy Nicholson.*

Other starting points:

Start at both ends and work toward the center. You can control the symmetry well this way

.

Start at the center back and work around toward the front. Leave an opening big enough for your head to go through. Pin the center of your cords to your knotting board and work first one side, then the other. (See diagram, right.)

Necklace rings can often be found in craft shops and your cords can be mounted directly on those rings. The cords can be mounted all around or just in the center. If carefully planned, several sets of pendants can be made to slip on and off the ring, to suit your mood or outfit.

Photo 55. Necklace. Sybil Fainberg started her polypropylene necklace in the center back and joined the two sides for a pendant effect in the front. *Sybil Fainberg*. Photo, *Seymour Bress*.

Photo 56. Shaped Neckpiece. Here's another necklace started in the back and worked toward the front. The ceramic pieces add interest to this crisp, prettily shaped piece. Navy cord. Ceramic pieces, *Debbie Hopkins*. *Marjorie Mills*.

Start at the bottom of the pendant part and work toward the back. To end a pendant started this way, you may use any of the three endings first mentioned: bead, button, or bar. If the pendant is large enough to fit over your head, you can end it by overlapping the ends and use the wrapping method to bind the ends together. (See Wrapping, chart on inside back cover.)

A good way to join two sennits coming from opposite sides, as on a necklace, is to clip the filler cords short from both sennits.

Using the outside cords from side A as new core cords, knot around these filler cords with the outside cords of side B. When the knotting is completed, bring the ends of the knotting cords into the center of the sennit. Jeanne Vernon's pendant is done this way.

Some necklaces have no beginning or end, or at least so they appear. Examine Jeanne Vernon's necklace below.

You'll probably get some additional ideas just by looking at the photographs in this book. As you work, still more ideas will surely occur to you.

Photo 57. Neckpiece. This neckpiece started on the round ceramic disc. It radiated out from here, went down, up and rambled all around. Jute. Ceramic pieces, *Ebby Malmgren. Trudy Nicholson.*

Photo 58. Pendant. In a deliberate attempt to avoid a fringe at the front center, Jeanne Vernon chose to start in the front and work her way around to the back. She ended the necklace so skillfully that it's impossible to see where the cords overlapped. *Jeanne Vernon.*

Earrings

Earrings can be made by mounting your cords on earring rings. If you use very fine cords, you may even try knotting within the loops.

Photo 59. Earrings. *Madge Schneider.*

Purses

It's possible to make a great variety of purses. There are casual, dressy, tote, and evening purses, for example some standard sizes are suggested on page 65. Here are some beginning, ending, and construction ideas. It's a good idea to make a full-size paper pattern before starting, to see if the size and shape are really what you want.

In terms of construction, one of the simplest purses is made out flat like this:

It is mounted on a very heavy cord or group of finer cords and knotted on a flat board. When the knotting is completed, the purse is folded in half and sewn together on the open side. The fringe from the front and back halves are then knotted together. Wrapping makes a neat ending for this kind of purse and also closes the bottom. A handle may be made of the same cords used to make the purse and stitched onto the purse.

Envelope purses may be made flat, too.

Upon completion of the knotting, fold the purse on the lines indicated in the diagram, and sew the front and back seams together. Purses may be started at the bottom or the top and have fringes, or have the ends tucked away. If gussets are desired, they may be made sepa-

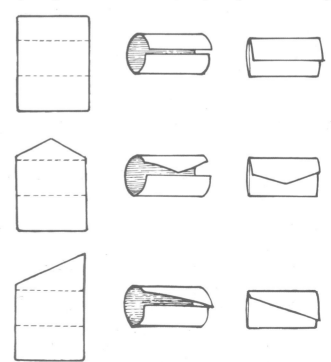

Photo 60. Twined and Knotted Purse. Doramay Keasbey has blended macramé and twining superbly in this handsome purse. *Doramay Keasbey.*

rately and stitched to the sides of the purse.

The body of a purse may be made in one piece by knotting it around a base. A good base, for example, is a polyurethane pad or pillow form.

Encircle the base with your mounting cord. Pin the cord directly onto the pad. Work from the top down. Rows of double half hitches make a firm and sturdy bottom or base for the purse. The ends may be brought inside and knotted together so that they won't pull out - or they may be fringed, or ended as the bottom of bottles. (See page 85.)

A purse may also be made in three pieces. The long strap will be used as the bottom of the purse, gussets, and straps.

Of course, purses can be started on purse handles. Dowels, bamboo rods, half-round moldings, rings, metal frames or wooden frames with a bar on which cords can be mounted all serve as good starting points for purses.

Conversely, a purse may be started from the bottom and may be mounted on a leather or wooden base.

One thing to watch for in making a purse is to be sure the opening is large enough for you to reach into it easily. When using bag handles, knot the back and the front separately for a few inches before starting to knot them together. You may also work the back and front separately, and then sew them together to within a few inches of the top.

If you make short sennits near the top of your purse, you can weave a cord over and under the sennits and make a drawstring purse.

Unless the knotting is very close, you'll probably want to line your purse. You might want to sew the lining directly to your purse or try the following idea.

Make a set of interchangeable, different-colored linings for your purse and secure them in place with Velcro, sturdy snaps or hooks and eyes. The character of your purse will change slightly with each different color, and the purse will blend with more of your clothes.

Photo 61. Tote Bag. Lola Liebner fashioned this handsome jute tote bag in four pieces - front panel, back panel, gusset for three sides, and handle. Courtesy Mrs. E. Lakin Phillips. *Lola Liebner.*

Photo 62. Ecuadorean Purse. The cords of this purse are mounted directly onto a simple, wooden handle. The back and front are knotted separately for about 1fi" and then joined at the sides. The cords are brought to the inside at the bottom and the purse is lined. Gift from *Allen Bress.*

Photo 63. Knapsack. Have you ever thought about making your own knapsack? Richard Mathews has, and has done so very successfully. *Richard Mathews.*

Photo 65. Meticulously constructed purse. It is ended with a few rows of double half hitches and a fringe. *Marie Grassi.*

Photo 64. Handwoven Purse with Macramé Overlay. The knotted handles on this purse are particularly versatile. They can be shortened or lengthened at the wearer's discretion or pleasure. *Richard Malmgren, M.D.* Photo, *Seymour Bress.*

Photo 66. Purse. Handsome, sturdy purse of cotton seine twine and wooden beads. Shown open. *Richard Mathews.*

Pillows

Pillows and purses are made in a similar fashion. As for pillows, here are some ideas.

You might do well to make a full-scale paper pattern of pillows too, to make sure they will suit your needs. Standard sizes are listed on the chart on page 65, but it is fun to vary these.

The easiest way to make a pillow is to do your knotting directly around the form on which the finished pillow will be mounted. You will be sure to knot it to the proper size this way. Square, rectangular, and round polyurethane pillow forms are available and these make good bases. Sometimes you can have forms cut to your specifications.

You can make a pillow on a flat board and fold it to shape when you're finished. Or, if a gusset is desired, make the back, front, and gusset separately and then stitch them together.

The end cords may be hidden in the lining by using any of the methods mentioned previously - or they may be used decoratively, as part of the design.

Mats

Now for some pretty place mats. Again, note the standard sizes as listed on page 65. Make a paper pattern of a shape that pleases you, and start knotting. Here are some shapes that work well with macramé.

Bottles

There's something intriguing about covering a bottle. First, let's start at the top and work down. For your first attempt, choose a bottle that has a good resting place for the starting cords near the top of the bottle. Cut your cords in multiples of four.

To Start: Take one of your cords and use it as a mounting cord. Pin it to your knotting board and hitch the rest of your cords onto it.

Now, remove all these cords from your knotting board and transfer them to your bottle.

Wrap the mounting cord around the "nesting place" in your bottle. To close the circle on your mounting cords, bring the right cord over the left cord and, holding the cords firmly, make a double half hitch onto the right cord with the left cord. Pull tight. Then, drop the two mounting cords and use them in your knotting pattern.

Knot in the pattern of your choice. If the bottle widens, you may want to add extra cords as you progress. See pages 55-57 for some methods of adding on cords.

The simplest way to end your bottle cover is to make a fringe near the bottle's base.

A particularly neat and satisfactory way of finishing the base (or bottom) of the bottle is to do row after row after row of double half hitches in spiral fashion, gradually decreasing the number of cords, until they are all used up.

Start with any two cords and use them as your knot bearers. Do about four complete double half hitches over these two knot bearers. Drop one knot bearer and cut it off short. Pick up another cord to replace the one you cut off, and do about four more double half hitches. Drop the oldest knot bearer, cut short, pick up another cord to replace it, and continue in this manner until all the cords are cut off. Work the last cord back under the other cords.

There is no hard and fast rule about how many double half hitches you do with each pair of knot bearers. Start with four. If you have many cords, you may have to reduce the number of double half hitches you do with

each pair of knot bearers. On the other hand, if you seem to be eliminating cords so fast that there may not be enough left to cover the bottom, do more than four double half hitches around each pair of cords.

Another way of ending the knotting is to have the knotting go right to the base of the bottle, and even a bit onto the bottom of the bottle. The cords can be trimmed and glued down. If this causes the bottle to become wobbly, a heavy piece of fabric, cardboard, or a thin piece of wood may be glued to the bottom.

Photo 67. Bottom View of Bottle. The cords were gradually decreased, as described in the text. The bottom is flat and the bottle doesn't wobble when standing. *Jeanne Vernon.*

Photo 68. Covered Bottle. The pattern intertwines in an interesting way. *Jeanne Vernon.*

To Hang A Bottle

Perhaps you'd like to hang a bottle, or a vase, a jar, or even a bowl. For this, you could start at the bottom and work up. When knotting from the bottom up, it may be easier to work with your bottle, jar or vase upside down. This is easy for wide-necked pieces, but what about a narrow-necked bottle? Well, try this, or devise your own ingenious method. Fill a tall, wide-necked jar or flower pot with sand or lightly crumpled newspaper or tissue paper. Insert the neck of your bottle into the jar, and adjust the sand or paper so that the bottle doesn't wobble.

The next thing you'll find is that you can't stick pins into a piece of glass. Tape can help you out of a temporary jam.

Here's one method of working:

Draw an outline of the bottom of your bottle and pin it to your knotting board. Pin a ring to the center of the outline. The ring must be smaller than the base of your bottle and large enough to accommodate the number of cords you're working with. Often 12 or 20 cords and an open knotting pattern are used in hanging pieces. Knot in sennits or in any pattern of your choice. When the knotting is wide enough to cover the bottom of your bottle, transfer the knotting from your board to your upside down bottle and continue knotting.

The following is a particularly good method if your knotting will be dense:

Draw an outline of the bottom of your bottle and pin it to your knotting board. Start in the center with a mounting cord in the same general shape as the bottom of your bottle. Work out from the center, increasing the number of cords as you go along. (For more specific instructions on how to do this, refer to the method for working circular pieces on pages 56-57.) When the knotting is large enough to cover the bottom of your bottle, transfer your work to your upside-down bottle. Knot around the bottle, decreasing near the neck, if desired.

When all of your knotting is completed, you'll want to join the ends so that the piece can be hung. The easiest, but not always prettiest, way to do this is to gather all your cords together and make one large overhand knot at the point where you'll be hanging your piece. Trim the ends.

Another way is to again gather all the ends. For this method, you'll probably have too many ends and if you used them all, your hanger would be too bulky. See if any can be cut off. The core cords of sennits can be cut close and won't weaken the piece appreciably if they are cut off. Overlap the remaining cords and bind them together by the wrapping method or by square knotting the ends together. Jeanne Vernon's pendant on page 79 uses the latter technique.

Photo 69. Hanging Bottle. This bottle is cradled in knotting that starts at the bottom and ends at the top. *Jeanne Vernon.*

To make a Loop:

Gather all the ending cords together. Make a sennit of square knots starting at about the height you'd like to hang your container. Fold the sennit over. Clip the core cords short. Make another square knot just beneath the first square knot in the sennit. Make a few more square knots. Work the ends back in or clip and glue the ends.

If you'd rather have two or more hanging loops, the cords can be split and wrapped in smaller groups.

Photo 70. Close-up of the loop formed for her hanging bottle. *Jeanne Vernon.*

Photo 71. (left) Here's another hanging container that was worked from the bottom up. The technique is the same as Jeanne's other bottle, but the knotting pattern is quite different. *Jeanne Vernon.*
Photo 72. (right) Flower Container. This glass flower holder has a bulit-in depression which comfortably houses a strip of shell knots. *Jeanne Vernon.*

Photo 73. Close-up of hanger for the container in Photo 72. *Jeanne Vernon.*

Photo 75. A clever, complex Hanger. See if you can figure it out! *Jeanne Vernon.*

Photo 74. Close-up of the flower container in Photo 72. *Jeanne Vernon.*

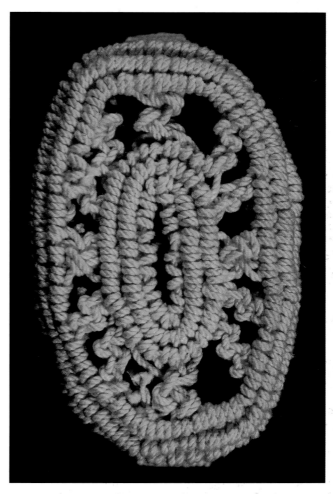

Photo 76. Bottom of Hanging Bottle in Photo 71. The knotting for this bottle was started in the center with an oval-shaped holding cord. Cords were added as needed to widen the knotting and cover the whole bottom. *Jeanne Vernon.*

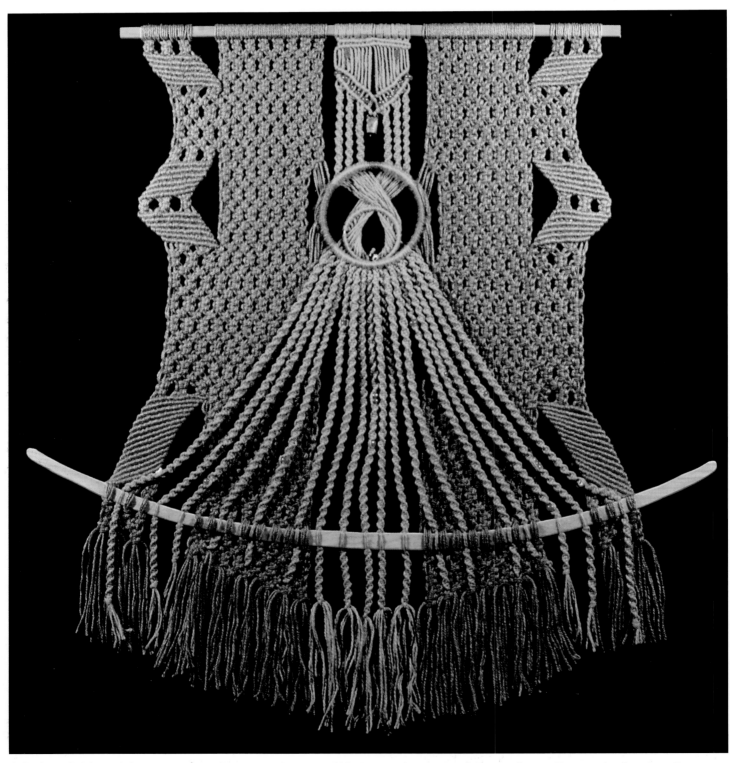

Chapter Five

Photo 77. Blue and green hanging. Made by request to go with a blue and green handwoven pile rug. Rug wools. Courtesy *Dan Bress. Helene Bress.*

Divine Inspiration: Design

Designing your own piece of work can be fun, agonizing, exciting, painful, exhilarating, or any combination of these. When the design works, and you've created something that's pleasing to you, the feeling is one of great pleasure.

There are many different approaches to the problem of design. The particular piece, combined with your own personality, will determine which approach you'll use.

If you've never designed anything on your own before, you may be timid about starting now. You may feel that the only thing you can do is to copy something you've seen. Artists and designers frown upon this, but sometimes it's helpful just to get you started. When you copy though, it is expected that you will give the original artist credit by saying, "Knotted by [*your name*], after an original by [*artist's name*.]"

The hope is that you'll only start by copying, and that you'll soon begin to change things - the color, order of knots, placement of beads, proportion, etc. - thus gradually designing your own work.

Sometimes you may just have a very vague idea of what you want to do. You must decide upon the kind of cords, color, approximate finished length, and how you want to start, but you don't have to have the design of the work well formed in your mind. You can just hitch on your cords, start working, and design the work as you go along. One idea usually leads to another. This is not to imply that as you knot one section, the next automatically forms under your fingers.

Photo 78. Close-up of Photo 77. The "evil eye" bead in the center wards off evil spirits! *Helene Bress.*

For some, it almost will; for others, it will require much thought. My feelings are that if you just do anything at all that pops into your head, your finished work will look as if you've just done anything at all that popped into your head, and you'll have an erratic, poorly designed work. If you stop occasionally, however, to consider the part you have completed and look back to see if a pleasing composition is forming, you are more likely to form a well composed, integrated work.

Of course, you can plan your work in advance, on paper or in your head, and proceed in this way. Even when you do have a specific idea, it is still wise to stand back every once in a while and evaluate what you have done to be sure that the next part will fit in as you planned.

In designing, there are many points to consider. For example, the materials and knotwork should be appropriate to the particular project. If you're making a stole, the materials should be relatively soft and the knotting open so that the stole will drape well. That combination would be disastrous for a knapsack, however.

Color needs to be handled with discretion in macramé. If different-colored cords are used in adjacent areas, the effect can become very cluttered or muddy looking. Color can be used effectively by keeping the color areas distinct and clear. Colors can be added to a work with beads, twining, Ghiordes or rya knots and weaving. Also, colors can be hidden within

sennits and be made to emerge when desired. Colors can be made to appear and disappear in Cavandoli work, i.e., close work consisting of horizontal and vertical half hitches. (See page 43.)

Generally, a smooth, hard, twisted cord is used in macramé, and texture and surface interest is achieved with knots. A change of knotting pattern and areas of open spaces will change the texture. For special effects, feathers, beads, unusual yarns, and Ghiordes knots can be used.

Most often we think of macramé in terms of knotted areas and pay little attention to the open areas. Open areas with just a few, discreet knots can be very effective. Smaller open areas are important, too.

Can you visualize this - a large, irregularly shaped piece of driftwood, a sennit of square knots made with heavy natural jute, a pink satin ribbon attached to it, and all held together with a big rhinestone pin?

Surely that's unique, but is it pleasing? Is it good design? Sometimes it becomes very important to us to create something different. To be successful, I think it should be pleasing as well. "Pleasing," however, is in the eye of the beholder. My hypothetical driftwood-jute-satin-rhinestone is a horror to me, but may be someone else's delight. The important thing is, though, that it be pleasing to you and not just different.

Execution is not directly a design concern. I insert it here, however, because I believe that poor workman-

Photo 79. Dress (detail). This dress is made with a tightly knotted yoke, cuffs, and hem, and free-flowing yarn in between. For the sake of modesty, it's been lined. *Mary Belle Frey.*

Photo 80. Wall Hanging. The open areas play as important a part as the knotted ones. A few wooden beads and shower curtain rings are added for color and design interest. Made of heavy cotton seine twine. *Marion Roscheck.*

Photo 81. Wall Hanging. *Ella Bolster.*

ship can spoil an otherwise good design. Extemporaneous sloppiness is sometimes encouraged as an art form, but it seldom comes off successfully. For example, if some cords become too short to be used, you can let them hang where they will and incorporate them into your design. I think that you should take a good look at your work and/or your conscience however, and decide whether the cords are hanging there for beauty - or because of laziness.

When you become interested in an art or craft, you see ideas for designs almost everywhere. At first, though, you may wonder how you'll ever think of things to make and where you'll get good design ideas for them. After a while you'll wonder how you're ever going to complete all your prospective projects and ideas in just one lifetime. You also begin to collect strange assortments of things and justify your bizarre behavior by saying, "It will be just perfect for the next piece I do," or, "It's my only vice."

While leafing through a magazine in the dentist's office, I came upon a picture of a lovely church. The more I looked at it, the more ways I saw of interpreting it in macramé. I can't reproduce that one for you to see, but do offer this one for your contemplation: a magnificent Norwegian Stave church. Photo courtesy *Horace M. Johnson.*

Architectural shapes are often adaptable to macramé. Modern buildings, old buildings, castles, and churches from different countries are all worth observing.

Sometimes paintings, or a part of a painting, may spark an idea in you.

Forms and materials from nature can be good sources of inspiration. The shape of a plant or an animal may be used directly as in some of the illustrations, or abstractly. Natural materials, such as shells, driftwood, and feathers can be incorporated directly into a piece.

Seashells can be used in many ways. Holes can be poked into some with a sharp pointed object or shells can be knotted into pieces as described in the section on enclosing objects, or used as in the necklaces on the following page.

The neckpiece incorporating shells that Paul Johnson knotted has quite a different feel to it. (See Photo 140.) And the form of the shell itself can inspire a whole piece of macramé.

"Found Objects" may inspire a project: those miscellaneous nothings that you collect because you can't pass them up. They're pretty, or useful, or unusual, or have sentimental value, and will surely come in handy someday.

Photo 82. Driftwood. Driftwood was the starting point for this dramatic piece. *Jeanne Vernon.*

Photo 83. Neckpieces. Trudy Nicholson made this pair of jute neckpieces for good friends. The oyster shells were carefully selected from a great heap of shells. These necklaces were among her first projects! *Trudy Nicholson.*

I found some wooden hoops in an antique shop, and immediately began to think in circles. Friends were intrigued with the same idea, and working completely independently of one another we came up with these creations.

The technical approach, the materials used, and the designs for each of these are quite different, but each person tried to keep the motion of the circle, each in her own way.

While still on this hoop-circle binge, I spotted a basket-ball hoop in a department store. I looked at my husband. He did some fast mind-reading and said, "No." So we took it home...

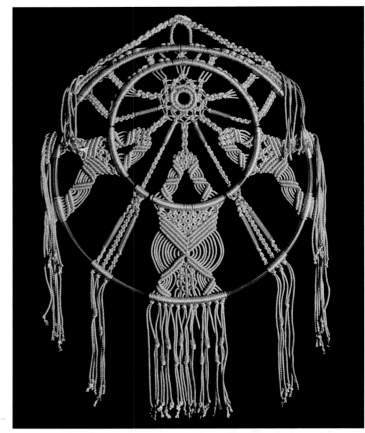

Photo 85. Knots in Orbit. During one of the moon flights, Ella Bolster created these Knots in Orbit. She started with the innermost hoop and worked her way out, adding hoops and yarns along the way. Her moon-age materials are all synthetic - plastic hoops, plastic beads, and white nylon yarn. *Ella Bolster.*

Photo 84. Circular Hanging. Doramay Keasbey completely covered her hoop and worked from the top, around and down. She used natural cotton seine twine and two cork floats - seagoing materials. *Doramay Keasbey.*

Photo 86. Basketball Net. Yes, my sons will use it! It's made of gold and green nylon seine twine so that it will withstand hard wear and weather. *Helene Bress.*

Photo 87. Circular Hanging. Only my circular piece is earthbound. I started in the general vicinity of the North Pole, went on down South, and crossed over Equator-wise. I used a rough wooden hoop, natural India jute, brown and orange linen, and an antiquated brass bell. *Helene Bress.*

A friend of Trudy Nicholson's wanted a macramé setting for her hand-carved ivory pendant from Nepal. See how Trudy resolved this design problem.

Photo 88. This is a hand-carved ivory pendant from Nepal and its owner wanted a macramé setting for it.

Photo 89. A comfortable and very suitable home for the Nepalese pendant. The setting is complete in its own right. It has a built-in hook for the ivory pendant to hook on to, and spaces where the pin back will fit. The ivory piece may be taken on or off at will. *Trudy Nicholson.*

Photo 90. Macramé setting with ivory pendant. Here's the setting with the pendant in place. *Trudy Nicholson.*

Consider some of these as headings for a wall hanging: an ornamental drawer pull, a key chain, unusual belt buckles, bamboo, an Israeli oil lamp, toe rings, boomerang, chopsticks, bamboo flute, dowels, moldings, knitting needles, rug shuttle, plastic bars, ceramic pieces, turned pieces from discarded furniture, embroidery hoops, clock handles.

Once you start looking, you'll probably find design ideas in the most unlikely places and at the most unlikely times - perhaps while feeding peacocks at the zoo or while idly watching shadow patterns on the floor.

Photo 91. Lobster. Hannelies Penner saw a piece of silver jewelry that was made in a shape similar to this. It intrigued her and she began studying pictures in children's books and in art magazines. She then put the pictures aside and made a sketch of her own. This lovely pendant is the result of her efforts. *Hannelies Penner.*

Photo 92. Hanging. Using a bamboo flute as a top piece, Connie Brown handled a potential design problem very deftly. The flute didn't lend itself to having many cords mounted onto it. When a knotted piece starts with a small number of cords, it is usually narrow at the top and gets wider as it goes along. That's fine if that's the shape you want. If it isn't, however, study Connie's treatment for another idea. *Connie Brown.*

Photo 93. Wall Hanging. Open, flowing, and rhythmical. *Lola Liebner.*

Photo 94. Acrobats. Here the human form is portrayed playfully and successfully. *Linda Hendricks.*

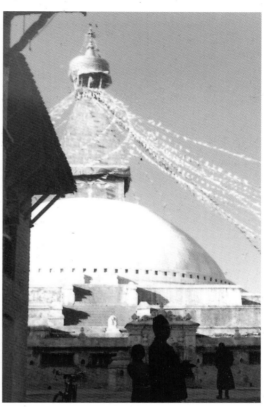

Photo 96. Nepalese Church. When in Nepal, Trudy Nicholson was quite impressed with this Buddhist Temple, or Stupa. It sits on top of a hill, all by itself, and is quite a conrast to its surroundings. Courtesy *Trudy Nicholson.*

Photo 95. Pendant. Trudy Nicholson captures the lines and spirit of the lovely Nepalese church in her pendant. *Trudy Nicholson.*

Photo 97. Back view of pendant to show the technical details of how the stone was enclosed. *Trudy NIcholson.*

Chapter Six

Photo 98. Macramé hanging with a little twining and wrapping. *Helene Bress.*

Widening Horizons:
unique ways with macramé

The marriage of different techniques often results in unique and pleasing effects. There is nothing new about the following techniques in themselves. Their use with macramé, however, helps to give macramé a new dimension.

Wrapping

We have discussed the wrapping technique before, but only in reference to ending pieces. It does make a neat ending, but can also be used decoratively within a piece. (See Diagram on inside back cover.)

As we have seen, adding new, clear-cut areas of color in macramé is sometimes a problem. One of the nicest things that wrapping can do for you is to allow you to add spots of new color wherever you choose. I think that the little gold linen hanging (opposite page) helps to illustrate the point.

The basic knotted portion is all of a deep gold color and it includes some burnt-orange beads. This color scheme was carried one step further with a woven area and again with some wrapping below it.

Groups of cords were wrapped with different colors and textures of yarns, and this added textural interest to the piece. Yarns used for wrapping were gold and orange linen and rusty-orange and deep olive rug wool. Some more knotting, a few more beads, and then the piece was ended with wrapped fringes. The same colors as before were used for the bottom fringe, but in a somewhat different order.

Edwina Drobny's uses wrapping freely and effectively.

Photo 99. Necklace. Linen, wool, sand dollars, and pewter. *Edwina Droby.*

Rya or Ghiordes Knot

The Ghiordes knot is a very common knot to rug makers, and one that can add new dimensions to your macramé. It is one of the most widely used knots for making a pile surface, such as long-pile rya rugs and short, clipped flossa rugs. Handweavers often use it to create surface texture on purses, pillows, or wall hangings. Knotters can adapt it for their needs, too. As you can see from the photo below, the Ghiordes knot enriches the surface of the knotting with an interesting texture.

Photo 100. Close up. White Hanging with Ghiordes Knots. Rayon and wool blend yarn. Unglazed stoneware beads made by the artist. 16" x 39". *Paul Johnson.*

Let's do a few Ghiordes knots to see how it works.

Soft yarns such as knitting yarns and rug yarns, work well. They can be combined with other yarns such as fine cottons and linen to give interesting effects.

For a sample: Cut six cords, each two feet long. Use any cord you would usually use for macramé projects. Fold them in half and mount them on a knotting cord or stick.

Instructions: With the first four cords (using two core cords and two knotting cords) make one square knot.

Cut three strands of knitting yarn, each six inches long. Keep them together as if they were just one strand of yarn.

Center the three strands over the two core cords of the square knot.

Bring the strands on the left around and under the left-hand core cord.

Bring the three strands on the right around and under the right-hand core cord.

Push the ends up or pin them to your knotting board to keep them out of the way while you do the next step.

Make a square knot directly below the Ghiordes knot. This will hold the Ghiordes knot in place.

For practice, continue this across the row and then experiment with various combinations and patterns of square knots and Ghiordes knots.

The ends of the Ghiordes knot can be left long, or clipped rather short - or used in a combination of the two. New colors can be added to your macramé piece freely and easily in this way. Ghiordes knots can be clumped together in great quantities or spaced far apart and used sparingly. Most often several strands of yarn are used together to make a Ghiordes knot. These strands can all be of one color and material, or they may be of a few colors and different materials.

This technique is especially suited for use in decorative pieces such as wall hangings and pillows, and perhaps purses and necklaces. With appropriate materials, you could even make a rug!

Enclosing an Object

If an object has a hole in it, or can easily have a hole drilled into it, knotters eye it knowingly, and usually build a macramé piece around it. Unfortunately, there are some beautiful objects in this world that have no hole, and resist having one put into them. Don't despair. Perhaps you can use it by knotting around it. Here's my first attempt, and it failed. The problem I set out to solve was to enclose a pretty-colored shell disc into a piece of knotting without putting a cord through it. I chose navy cord to work with. If you've ever worked with navy cord, you know that although it knots well, it is stiff and has a strong will.

Well, the disc refused to stay lodged where I put it. If the disc were more tapered and the cord a bit more cooperative, the idea might have worked. I put square knots directly above and below the disc, leaving the core cords behind the disc, and the knotting cords in front of it. Good idea, but when it was finished the disc slipped out. I admitted defeat, undid the bottom square knots, slipped a cord through the hole in the top of the disc, and proceeded as before. It held this time, but a little reluctantly. The skips in the cords are long and they don't always stay lined up where I meant them to.

Photo 101. The Attempt that Failed. *Helene Bress.*

Photo 102. Close-up of a section of a wall hanging, "To Harry." This round, glass float is securely locked in place with overhand knots in strategic places. *Madge Schneider.*

We learn from our mistakes as well as our successes.

It will be impossible to set down the exact directions telling you how to enclose a particular object. I'll put down some starting points and hints, and hope that with this, and a little of your own ingenuity, you'll be able to cope with problems your own treasures may present.

I've selected a flat, round, enameled disc for this first sample and some heavy cotton cord so that you'll be able to follow the knots in the photograph easily. In the hardware store I found a ring that is just slightly smaller than the disc. The disc was set aside temporarily, and the ring

pinned to the knotting board. A few cords were folded in half and mounted to the ring with double half hitches. *Please note carefully:* All the cords were hitched onto the ring with double half hitches.

The next cords were worked like this:

The first half of a pair was hitched right next to the other cords.

The second half was brought to the opposite side of the ring and hitched onto it there.

A few more cords were double half hitched onto the ring.

Another pair was then broken up as before. The first half was hitched on alongside the others; the other half was hitched on directly opposite to it.

Then the enameled disc was put into place behind the ring, and under the crossed cords. More cords were hitched on and one more crossover was made on the back of the disc.

The enameled disc is now being held in place quite firmly. The cords can now be used to make a choker, a necklace, bracelet, or belt. They can also radiate and be made into a circular piece.

The object could also be worked into a piece that is being worked from the top down. When you reach the point where you want to enclose your object, hitch your ring on as you would hitch on a new holding cord. After a few double half hitches are completed, begin to criss-cross some cords on the back as before.

You can't always find a ring the right size for your object, and a purchased ring may be too thick to be in character with the rest of your piece. Also, you may want to start with a different shape, one which more closely resembles the shape of your object. If you do, you can fashion your own mounting piece out of wire. Copper wire is readily available in hardware stores.

Bend the wire in your hands to the shape you want. Check to be sure that it's slightly smaller than the object you plan to enclose. Overlap the ends of the wire generously and twist them lightly around each other a few times to hold the shape closed. (Pliers might come in handy if you are using a thick wire.) Mount your knotting cords onto this with double half hitches and continue as before.

Photo 103. Front and back view of a flat enamel disc that has been firmly enclosed into a piece of macramé.

Enclosing a Three-Dimensional Item

A three-dimensional item can be incorporated into a piece of macramé, too. In this case, you will probably want to be able to see as much of the piece as possible - the sides as well as the top.

Again you can start with a ring or form a shape out of wire to conform to the shape of your object to be enclosed. Of course, your starting piece will have to be slightly smaller than the piece being enclosed. For a sample, and trial run, I chose a relatively regular seashell, a ring slightly smaller than the top of the shell, and some heavy cotton cord. This will illustrate the technique, and then we'll go on to more complex situations.

To wrap up this seashell:

Pin the ring to a knotting board.

Mount cords onto the ring with double half hitches.

Make sennits of square knots, or other knots if you prefer, using core cords.

When the sennits are long enough to reach from the top of the shell to the bottom of it, remove the knotting from the board.

Turn it upside down and put the shell in place. Bring the core cords from one of the sennits under the shell, to a sennit on the opposite side.

Make a square knot around this cord.

Repeat this procedure several times until the shell is securely locked in.

Continue knotting as desired.

Photo 104. Sample of one method of enclosing a three-dimensional object.

Now that the simpler forms of enclosing are understood, let's discuss enclosing an irregularly shaped object. When you reach this point, you may need to inject some imagination and ingenuity into the situation.

Almost certainly you'll want to shape your own starting piece out of wire. Keep in mind that wire shapes can be worked effectively into any natural crevices or depressions in the piece. Next, you'll need to mount some cords, but because you'll want the sides of your piece to show, you won't want to mount them densely. Well, you can just double half hitch some cords on at intervals around the wire. If you want to cover the wire completely, double half hitch some cords on and where you want a space, yet want to cover the wire, make a third half hitch - and maybe a fourth and fifth - with the same cord.

You have covered the wire, yet left a space.

After the cords are mounted, knot in a design, using any knots that please you. When the pattern of knots is long enough to reach from the top of your object to the base of it, take your knotting off your board and turn it upside down. Put your object in place. Now you want to keep this object from falling out. If you have sennits of square knots, you can switch core cords as before and secure it in place this way.

If you have double half hitches, just take a knotting cord from one side as in the earlier sampler, bring it across to the other side and use it as an additional knotting cord on this side. Do this as many times as necessary to secure the object in place.

Photo 105. Bracelet. The problem was to enclose a large, tumbled stone in a piece of macramé so that the stone would be secure, yet have a great deal of its surface exposed. The solution: this exquisitely designed bracelet. In designing the enclosure, Mary Belle Frey followed the natural markings in the stone. *Mary Belle Frey.*

Photo 106. Close-up of the underside of the bracelet. The waxed linen cord is very strong and these few cross-overs will hold the stone in place. *Mary Belle Frey.*

Photo 107. Close-up of a section of the hanging "To Harry." A simple way to enclose an object. The knotting cords are lodged in the natural crevices of the shell. *Madge Schneider.*

Photo 108. Leather Case for Small Etchings. Leather, linen, and wood. *Edwina Drobny.*

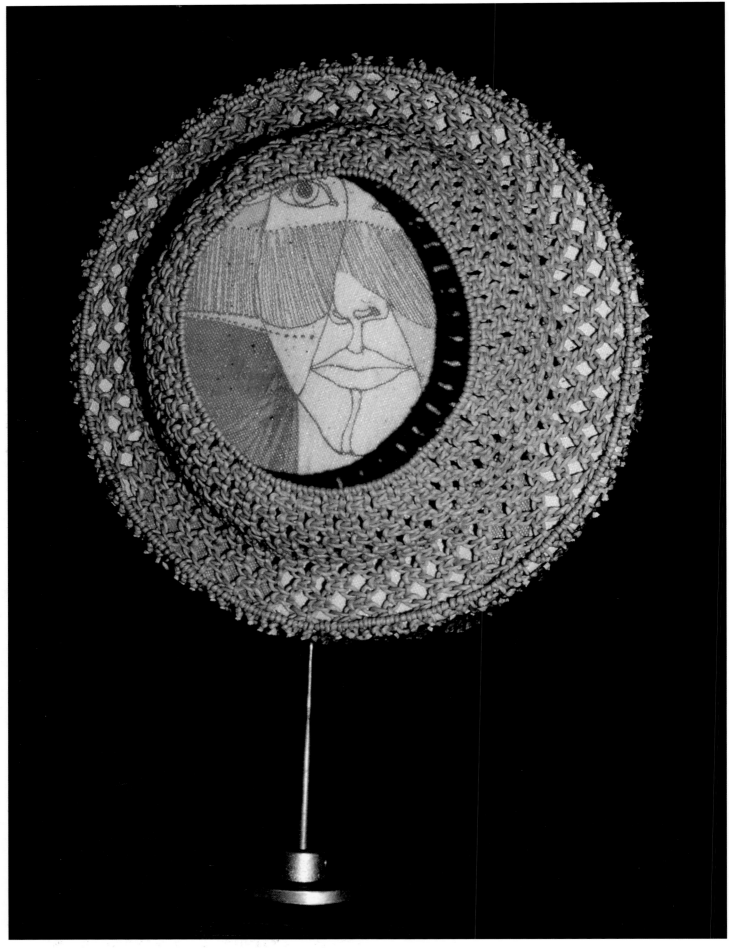

Chapter Seven

Photo 109. Table Sculpture. Linen, etching on canvas stretched over steel frame. *Edwina Drobny.*

Combining Craft Techniques

As craftsmen grow within their field, they often reach out toward other crafts as well. Also craftsmen tend to know and associate with other artists and craftsmen. Combining different crafts and arts is a natural outcome of both of these occurrences. Macramé combines well with many different arts - weaving, ceramics, leatherwork, enameling, sculpture, jewelry-making, woodworking, knitting, crocheting, stitchery, and sometimes even painting.

In combination, sometimes the macramé will assume only a utilitarian or decorative role. At other times, the knotting will be the focal point, with the other techniques used as decorative accents, and sometimes there is a complete marriage of the two.

Let's take a look at some pieces which are a combination of knotting and another medium.

Weaving and Macramé

It seems strange to extol the virtues of combining weaving and macramé within one piece as if today we are doing something brand new since it is possible that macramé was first used in this way. Well, this is still a good way to combine the two crafts. The warp threads are the threads that go vertically on a loom. Usually, it was these threads that were used to knot with after a piece was completed. However, weft threads which are woven across the warp, can be used too, as we'll soon see.

We don't all have the elaborate equipment and weaving skill needed to make some of the examples of weaving and macramé combinations shown here. If you like the effect of this combination though, you could try the following:

Buy a piece of fabric, hem it to the size you desire, add threads onto this, and knot the ends. Attractive

Photo 110. Handwoven Mexican Blouse. Simple, handwoven cotton blouse, with decorative edgings of macramé on the sleeves and bottom edge. Long weft threads were deliberately woven in and left hanging at the sleeve part and long warp ends left at the bottom so that the knotting could be done. Courtesy, *Sylvia Hoffman.*

stoles, runners, and belts are some articles that can be made in this way.

Choose a fabric with a relatively loose weave.

Cut your cords as long as necessary. They will be halved, so account for this in your calculations. (For example, a single cord 24 inches long will become two 12-inch cords when mounted on your fabric.) Insert the cords in the cloth in this manner:

Fold your cord in half.

Ease a crochet hook between some threads in the fabric and hook the cord onto it.

Gently bring the cord through the fabric. Bring the free ends through the loop, and tighten.

Continue in this way until all your cords are hitched on, and then knot in your pattern.

Martha Hoering's method of warping, or setting up the frame loom, is unique and particularly suited for combining the weaving with macramé. When Martha finished the weaving part, she handed the project over to me. I removed the woven hanging from the canvas stretcher, pinned the bottom dowel to my knotting board and then blithely knotted away. I kept reminding myself that the knotting must be in keeping with the rest of the hanging. I became very involved with the knotting and perhaps the knotting became too involved! (See photo 114.)

Photo 112. Hanging. Combining weaving and macramé. The dowels are both functional and decorative. 10/5 linen was used. *Ella Bolster.*

Photo 111. Top view of Pandora's Box. Vertical and horizontal double half hitches. *Susan Gable Williamson.*

Photo 113. Side view Pandora's box. The top is done in macramé and the sides are woven. *Susan Gable Williamson.*

Ceramics and Macramé

Ceramics and macramé work beautifully together.

Photo 114. The combined effort of three good friends. Weaving on a canvas stretcher frame loom. *Martha Hoering*. Knotting, *Helene Bress*. Ceramic bead, *Ebby Malmgren*.

Photo 115. Clay Mirror with Macramé. Ebby Malmgren made this ceramic mirror blank, and incised a few slits into it. Just a touch of macramé and a few of Ebby's handmade beads were added to it. *Ebby Malmgren, Helene Bress*.

Other Art Forms and Macramé

Other art forms lend themselves well to combining them with macramé. For example, Edwina Drobny does a superb job of combining handwrought metalwork with macramé to make especially handsome jewelry.

Photo 116. Collar. Linen, pewter, and colored onyx. *Edwina Drobny.*

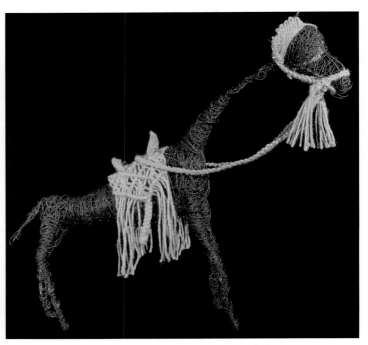

Photo 118. Don't look to Madge Schneider to separate media. This time she's dressed up her wire sculpture giraffe with a knotted jute bridle and saddle! *Madge Schneider.*

Photo 117. Fish. If there were a beauty contest for fish, this one would certainly take the prize. Connie Kazen created a very graceful, flowing, three-dimensional fish. She drilled holes into a plexiglass background in the general shape of the fish, hitched on some cords, and knotted down with the top cords and over toward the tail with the bottom cords. She used white navy cord which she painted after the fish was completed. *Connie Kazen.*

Photo 119. Leather and Macramé Hanging. May Shields cut free form shapes out of leather and designed this jute wall hanging around them. They look as if they were made for each other - and they were! *May Shields*.

Photo 120. Fire Screen Panel. This is the first of a series of panels to be used as a fire screen. The macramé and enameling blend well together. Macramé, *Melissa Diamanti*. Enameling, *the Diamanti Family*.

Chapter Eight

Photo 121. Strip Sampler. In this photograph some ends are left untrimmed so that construction details can be observed. In strip No. 11 new knot-bearing cords have been added below the angled parts in order to keep the symmetry of the colors. In strip No. 12 the beginning of the contrasting cord is not yet trimmed. (See diagram on page 118.) *Helene Bress.*

Spreading the Word

We warned you before, you chose to ignore the warning, and now you're highly contagious, ready to spread your mania to other unwarned, unsuspecting souls. Let's see if we can be of some help. Exciting things happen when you teach macramé. Often, you start with a timid but hopeful group. They're sure it's going to be very complicated, but are hopeful that they'll learn. With a little guidance, they find that it's not really very complicated after all, and almost immediately they are happily knotting away.

Among the most common words a teacher hears is, "I have no talent," "I can only copy things," "I have no color sense." Certainly some people have more talent than others, but most people have at least some artistic ability. When a teacher successfully encourages his students to reach out and try his wings, it is very gratifying for both student and teacher.

As a teacher, your enthusiasm is contagious; your patience very much appreciated.

Different situations require different methods of approach. Here are a few concrete suggestions.

Using a Strip Sampler

After teaching for a while using the method on pages 121-124, I became aware of many limitations inherent in its use. In an effort to make the teaching-learning experience a more vibrant and versatile one, I worked out the Strip Sampler method of teaching. As I thought about it, so many possibilities occurred to me that I couldn't wait to make several different kinds of this type of sampler myself - and to spread the word to others.

Here's the first sampler of this kind that I made. The strips were made in the order as numbered in the sketch on the following page. As you can see, the strips go from the simple to the more complex one step at a time. Each strip, in order, builds upon the knowledge learned in previous ones.

Some people come to the first class knowing a knot or two, some know none. Some people are quick to learn and work easily with their hands, others are slower. With the Strip Sampler, each can progress at his own speed. More or fewer strips can be made according to the time available and the ability of the individual. It is hoped that everyone will master the basics, but some of these strips are just variations that are fun to know, and not absolutely necessary.

The strips are done in a variety of materials. This gives students a chance to see what materials are available and how different materials work. The cords used are relatively short and the students prepare them quickly in class.

Diagram of Strip Sampler showing the order in which the strips were made. This it the key to the photo on page 116.

Colors are used and students see from the very beginning many ways in which color can be used successfully in macramé. The possibilities are endless - and the chances of any two people having identical hangings are quite remote.

Here are the vital statistics for the various strips as shown on my hanging. The space between the dowels is 14". The chart is arranged in the order in which the strips are taught.

Since this sampler will probably be used as a wall hanging, the student also is immediately concerned with color coordination and design. These need not be overwhelming concerns, however, because the strips can be rearranged and some can even be discarded, or repeated for accent, or redone in a more suitable color.

The strips are started in class, but only partially finished there. As soon as the student demonstrates that he can go on independently, he can stop, go on to something else, and finish the strips at home.

In design, the hanging can be very controlled, very free or anything in-between. The strips can all be the same length as in the first example, or like the diagrams on page 120.

The strip sampler can be started on a dowel, brass or plastic rod, hoop, flat stick, curtain rod, etc., but the heading should be even and smooth so that the strips can be rearranged if necessary. The endings can be varied, too, but should suit the character of the rest of the piece.

Key to Strip Sampler Diagram

1. Double Half Hitch: Horizontal and Oblique
Colors: 2 Ends: 8
Main Color:
  3 cords, each 4 yards long
Contrasting Color:
  1 cord 4 yards long

2. Diamond: crossing over center
Colors: 3 Ends: 14
Main Color:
  4 cords, each 4 yards long
Secondary Color:
  2 cords, each 4 yards long
Third Color (center):
  1 cord 4 yards long

3. Spiral: Half Square Knot with right cord over left
Colors: 1 Ends: 4
Core cords:
  1 cord 2 yards long
Knotting Cord:
  1 cord 6 yards long

4. Spiral - Half Square Knot, with left cord over right, plus beads. Spiral twirls in opposite direction to #3.
Colors: 1 Ends: 4
Core Cords:
  1 cord 2 yards long
Knotting Cords:
  1 cord 6 yards long

5. Whole Square Knot, combines the knots in #3 and #4
Colors: 1 Ends: 4
Core Cords:
  1 cord 2 yards long
Knotting Cords
  1 cord 4 1/2 yards long

6. Variations with Square Knot, 2 colors, core cord showing, overhand knot and bead combination
Colors: 2 Ends: 4
Core Cords (contrasting color):
  1 cord 2 yards long
Knotting Cord (main color):
  1 cord 4 1/2 yards long

7. Square Knot with Picot
Colors: 1 Ends 4
Core Cords:
  1 cord 2 yards long
Knotting Cords:
  1 cord 6 yards long

8. Square Knot with one type of Raised Picot
Colors: 1 Ends 4
Core Cords:
  1 cord 4 yards long
Knotting Cords
  1 cord 9 yards long

9. Alternating Square Knots
Colors: 1 Ends 12 or 16
If cords are fine:
  cut 8 cords 4 yards each
If cords are heavy:
  cut 6 cords 4 yards each

10. Diamonds with various knots in center.
Colors: 1 Ends: 16
Cut 8 cords, each 4 yards long

11. Angling. Two colors used so that the movement of colors can be observed. No need to copy this pattern exactly.
Colors: 2 Ends: 8
First Color:
  2 cords, each 8 yards long
Second Color:
  2 cords, each 8 yards long

12. Vertical Half Hitch combined with Horizontal Half Hitch to form a pattern (Cavandoli)
Colors: 2 Ends: 12
Main Color:
  6 cords, each 7 yards long
Contrasting Color:
  1 cord 13 yards long. This cord is *not* doubled over. If more design area is desired, make this cord longer.

I think it is important to teach all of the above in a basic course. If time permits, the following can be included as well

13. Josephine Knot
Colors: 1 Ends: 4
2 cords, each 4 yards long

14. Double Chain Knot
Colors: 2 Ends: 4
Color One:
  1 cord, 4 yards long
Color Two:
  1 cord, 4 yards long

15. Square Knot with colors interchanged
Colors: 2 Ends: 4
Color One:
  1 cord 4 yards long
Color Two:
  1 cord 4 yards long

16. Endings - various ways to end projects
  No new cords are needed - except for short lengths to wrap with.

On my personal list of things to do, are samplers of this sort:

An elegant one - with yarns such as rattail, soutache, and gold lamé, and accented with some beads made of porcelain or semi-precious stones.

A tiny one with thin, fine cords.

A big, bulky one of heavy jute, accented with hand-made ceramic beads and cork floats.

When using this strip sampler method, I usually have five sessions at weekly intervals and each session lasts two and one-half hours. My classes average from four to six people. I start everyone on the first strip together - and watch for problems and questions. When I feel that someone is quite comfortable and confident with the particular knot or technique, I suggest that he finish that strip at home and go on to the second strip. I start him off, still watching for the others. If someone is particularly quick, I give him some of the optional strips or other variations to work on. If someone is particularly slow, I'll have him skip some of the less important variations. In this way, the class progresses from one type of knotting to another at approximately the same time, and the most important procedures are covered by all. The last session is usually reserved for finishing techniques.

At the first session, I have out:

A knotting board and pins for each person. Scissors.

Dowels or plastic rods.

A yardstick and measuring board.

An assortment of yarns in many colors, usually one type of yarn predominating, however.

The first strip will set the tone for the rest of the sampler.

At the second session, I add some beads to the above collection, and some other types of yarns. I encourage each one to sample various kinds of yarn.

In the remaining sessions, the same materials are generally used.

It's always of great interest to students to see finished macramé pieces, as well as books and periodicals on the subject, lists of suppliers, samples of different yarns, slides and to know about exhibits that may be in town. I try to have these things and information available for students to study at the beginning and end of sessions.

Vertical Sampler

Here's another type of sampler that can be used as a basis for class sessions.

The same logical one-step-building-upon-the-previous-step order is followed as before. It works well, but is somewhat less versatile than the first one and is more tedious to set up.

When I use this method, I usually have four to five class sessions at weekly intervals and each session lasts from two to three hours. I keep the classes small - from four to six people.

Before the first class meets, I prepare for it by measuring and cutting the cords for each sampler. I use a different type of yarn and color for each sampler and hope that each person will find a set of cords that appeals to him. Each individual sampler is made in one color with only one type of yarn. In practice, I actually prepare several more packets of cords than there are people in the class, so that there will be more of a choice.

I use the following measurements for my vertical sampler but always run out of cord number 1 somewhere along the way. When I do, I take the opportunity to teach splicing methods. If you don't want to run out of cord, add ten yards to the measurement of that cord.

I start with: 16 cords, each eight yards long. Since these are halved when mounting, I wind up with 32 ends, each four yards long.

If the cords were not prepared in advance, the first session would be taken up by measuring, mounting, and shortening the cords. I feel that this would be a discouraging way to start.

As the students arrive, I have them choose a packet of cords, help them mount the cords on a starting piece, and teach them how to shorten the cords. We all work hard and fast so that everyone will have time to do two rows of horizontal double half hitches and the beginning of a diamond. Before the end of the first session, everyone understands how to form the diamonds, and some have completed them. Their homework is to complete the first two diamonds and do two more rows of horizontal double half hitches. If they have time, and choose to do so, they may make a second row of diamonds, or any similar pattern, and finish it off with another double row of horizontal double half hitches.

Within these relatively rigid limits, some of the more creative students come up with very interesting variations.

For the second session, I have on hand a good assortment of beads. I start out by teaching the spiral,

Photo 122. Vertical Sampler. *Helene Bress.*

Photo 123. Pendant. It's hard to believe, but this pendant started out as a class exercise. The arrow points to the starting point. If you turn the picture upside down, you can follow the knotting as it was done. When the back portion was completed, Trudy Nicholson turned it around, as pictured, and knotted the pendant portion adding threads as needed. Only a small portion of this was knotted in class. *Trudy Nicholson.*

or half square knot, and have the students leave groups of cords for the whole square knots and beads. After six of the spirals are completed, I teach the second half of the square knot, and have students select some beads. This is always a very interesting time for both the student and the teacher.

This is the first real opportunity for the student to inject a little of his own personality into his wall hanging. Usually, he sorts through the beads as if they were jewels - jewels he may have, but only a few - and so he must choose carefully. Sometimes this is the very first design experience for the student. How many beads should he choose, what color or colors, and in what order should he use them? I have strong ideas about these, but force myself to offer as few suggestions as possible. It usually pays off well. The student chooses what pleases him. He's really added something of his own to the project - and it usually looks well! Students often compare notes at this point, and are excited and inspired by the growth of the work around them.

After this section is completed another row of double half hitches are done in class if there is time. The principle of the alternating square knot is taught, and the next section is finished at home.

Up to this point, each student has been working with just one type of cord. I feel that it's important for students to try a variety of cords. For the third session I have them put their samplers to one side. I have out an assortment of yarn, and each one chooses something different from what he had been working with. They measure out six or eight cords, each cord two arm-lengths long and then mount them on a chopstick, dowel, or to their board with pins. I emphasize that this is just for practice, and won't be used for anything, but it often ends up as a necklace, bookmark, or some small piece anyhow.

Using these cords, I teach the raised picot, overhand knot, show how to add a stick and extra cords, and how to do the vertical half hitch. Sometimes there's time to teach the Josephine knot. I take extra cords for this.

This new little sampler is done extemporaneously and grows differently with each student. I try to have each person design his own somewhat, yet learn as many new things as possible. If you need to be more orderly than this, you can just follow the order as is shown in the large, pictured sampler. The home work for this session is to transfer the new techniques learned in class to the larger sampler. This may be done exactly like mine, or the student may design it in his own way. I always hope he'll design his own, but some students are still timid about this.

At the fourth session, all samplers are duly admired, questions are answered, and then the samplers are put aside once again. More cords are chosen this time, and two colors are used. I start with:

Two cords of color number 1 - each four yards long.

Two cords of color number 2 - each four yards long.

I have the students fold the cords in half and mount them on any small stick, or just with pins. I then teach them how to angle, using double half hitches, and go on to show the combination of horizontal and vertical half hitches and how to bring colors up at will (Cavandoli work). I spend the rest of the session teaching diamonds. Before the very end, we wrap the bottom cords. The homework is to complete the samplers at home incorporating these new techniques into them.

We're all sorry when a series of classes end, so a few former students formed a Macramé Guild. We meet once a month. I don't see the finished samplers at a formal class session, but do see them at these meetings. It's always a pleasant surprise. Usually, no two are alike, and some have even added their own hanger pieces on top.

Photo 124. Practice Sampler-Turned-Hanging. Started at the third class session and finished at home. *Ruth Gainer.*

Photo 126. (left). Another variation of the Vertical Sampler.
Photo 127. (right). Student Sampler. Here's Ruth Gainer's interpretation of the Vertical Sampler. She added ceramic beads and a ceramic top piece. Ceramic pieces, *Ebby Malmgren, Ruth Gainer.*

Photo 125a. (left) Sampler. Marion Roscheck chose to design her sampler from the very beginning. *Marion Roscheck.*
Photo 125b. (above) A student taught a student. Sampler by Trudy Nicholson's student, *Thais Weibel.*

Workshops

Once the basic knots and techniques are learned, students often enjoy attending workshops geared to one specific topic. Sometimes students suggest topics; sometimes you may have a pet idea you would like to get across. Here are some possibilities:

Jewelry

Covering a bottle or Enclosing an object

Making circular pieces

Christmas items

Necklaces

Purses

Chokers

Three-dimensional wall hangings

More knots - knots that have not been taught in class

Design: found objects

Making lampshades

Clothing

Belts

The approach you take will depend upon the particular topic you are working with. For a Christmas workshop, for example, you may want to have all the materials on hand and specific items to copy, whereas for a workshop on design using found objects, each student will probably be asked to bring his own found objects, and the design of the piece will evolve during the workshop.

To me, the amount of knotting accomplished in a workshop is the least important part of the workshop. A workshop is successful if people go home with new ideas, enthusiasm, and eagerness to try new approaches. If you are enthusiastic, know your topic, have some good examples on hand or pictures or slides to show, and have some good ideas stored in your head, you're bound to have a good workshop. Of course, there are some very practical matters that must be included, too, and if these are not taken care of, a workshop can just fall apart. For example, if you are supplying materials, you need to have enough materials on hand to go around.

Some Thoughts on a Christmas Workshop

For a Christmas workshop, several projects could be presented for the participants to interpret. Participants may start one or more projects and finish them at home. Their enthusiasm and imagination should be sparked by the workshop and they can interpret the ideas presented to suit themselves. For this type of workshop, appropriate materials need to be available. These may be supplied by the instructor or the participants could be asked to bring specific items.

Photo 128. Small dowels of graduated sizes, a few bells and a minimum of yarn are all that's needed for this simple tree. Variegated yarns work well for this. Size of this tree, 22"; any size can be made.

Photo 129. A three-dimensional tree this time. A clay top painted red (a ring could be substituted), embroidery hoops in graduated sizes, a few bells, and yarn are the materials needed. Green nylon seine twine was used for the basic knotting and bright red chenille and gold lamé for accents. Chenille doesn't knot well and so the chenille was twined below the first embroidery hoop and gently hitched onto the other hoops.

Chapter Nine

Photo 130. (left) Serenity. The front of this hanging is flat. The knots are simple and few, the hanging rather open. Marline twine, several weights of jute. 5' tall. Ceramic beads by *Ebby Malmgren. Helene Bress.*

Photo 131. (right) Serenity, back view. The sides and back of this hanging are rounded and the knotting is simple, but more concentrated than the front. It is constructed in this way so that when you view the front, the back forms a background that is not distracting. *Helene Bress.*

Artists at Work

H ere, now, is a gallery of fine work for your enjoyment. Seldom are more than the two basic macramé knots used in any of these pieces.

Wall Hangings

The creative artist often turns to wall hangings as a means of expression. Restrictions are fewest here and one's imagination can wander far afield.

Photo 132. Beginning of a Wall Hanging. The triangular shape that Beth Lister started with influenced the general form that this piece is taking. Purple cotton and rayon rug yarn. *Beth Lister.*

Photo 133. The Clothes Horse. Macramé over steel frame, painted canvas, and wood. *Edwina Drobny.*

Photo 134. Cylindrical Sculpture. Linen, wool, and forged pewter. *Edwina Drobny.*

Photo 135. "To Harry" Madge Schneider's designs grow as she works. She started with a piece of driftwood, some sea shells, glass floats, and polypropylene cord, and this complex interesting design evolved. *Madge Schneider.*

Photo 136. Solitude. This hanging starts in two dimensions and adds a third dimension along the way. Black upholsterer's cord, gold linen. About 2'. Ceramic pieces, *Ebby Malmgren. Helene Bress.*

Photo 137. Hanging. The colors seem to flow from one area to another in this hanging of many colors. *Augusta Petroff.*

Photo 138. Airy, open hanging. *Richard Mathews.*

Photo 139. Large, simple, dramatic hanging. Very heavy jute. 2 1/2 x 6 1/2'. *Peg Hardy.*

Photo 140. Money Cowry Necklace. Waxed linen, gold covered plastic beads, money cowry shells. Shells are held in place by tying a double overhand knot, placing glue on it, and pushing it into the opening in the back of the shell. *Paul Johnson.*

Photo 141. This is a very dainty piece done in heavyweight crochet cotton. It looks well hung against a wall or in front of a window with the light coming through. *Doramay Keasbey.*

Photo 142. Meticulously designed and executed wall hanging. Linen, about 10/5. *Ella Bolster.*

Photo 143. Close-up of a three-dimensional hanging. Of special interest is the cylindrical form within the outer, open circle of spiral sennits. Ceramic heading by Ebby Malmgren. *Sylvia Pocock.*

Photo 144. Here's one of Richard Mathews' more complex hangings. His double dowel mounting technique adds to the overall effect. *Richard Mathews.*

Jewelry

Photo 145. Earrings. Linen and beads. *Edwina Drobny.*

Photo 147. Earrings. Linen, cast pewter, wishbones. *Edwina Drobny.*

Photo 146. Necklace. Linen, wool, red onyx beads, red and purple tassels. *Edwina Drobny.*

Photo 148. Necklace. Linen, wool, and cast pewter. *Edwina Drobny.*

Photo 149. Pendant and Necklace. The pendant part of this necklace is detachable from the chocker. It is built on a gold colored wire that is shaped like a miniature hanger. Waxed linen, glass and wooden beads, gold color wire. *Paul Johnson.*

Photo 150. Gold Chocker-Bib. Gold elastic, blue faceted aurora borealis beads. *Paul Johnson.*

Photo 151. (top left) Egyptian Collar. Waxed linen with blue and white opaque pony and crow beads. 14" diameter. *Paul Johnson*.
Photo 152. (bottom left) Bib. Linen, wool, and forged pewter. *Edwina Drobny*.
Photo 153. (above) Nylon Braid Neckpiece. *Joan Michaels Paque*.

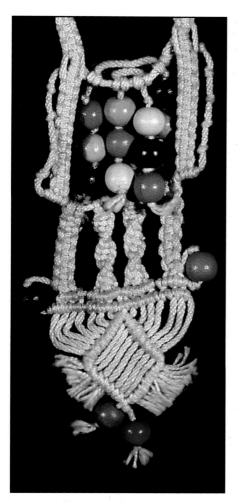

Photo 154. Necklace. *Jeanne Jarvis.*

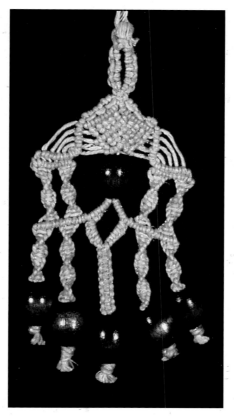

Photo 155. Pendant. *Doramay Keasbey*

Photo 156. Pendant. *Doramay Keasbey.*

Photo 157. Neckpiece. *Paul Johnson*

Photo 158. Choker. Waxed linen, glass and wooden beads. *Paul Johnson.*

Photo 159. Peacock Pendant. In Eastern folk art the peacock is interpreted in unique ways. Using peacock colors and memories of the folk art Hannelies Penner created this pendant. *Hannelies Penner.*

Photo 160. Necklace. *Paul Johnson*

Photo 161. Choker. Waxed linen, glass beads, ring neck pheasant feathers. Owner: *Jennifer Wyckoff. Paul Johnson.*

Miscellaneous

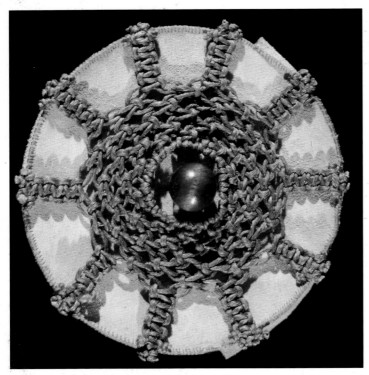

Photo 162. Leather case for Small Etchings. Leather, linen and wood. *Edwina Drobny.*

Photo 163. Red, white and blue flags were the design source for this pillow. Vertical and horizontal double half hitches were knotted on the face of the pillow, and sometimes on the reverse side to vary the texture. *Hannelies Penner.*

Photo 164. Covered Bottle. *Doramay Keasbey.*

Photo 165. Bell Pull. *Jeanne Jarvis.*

Photo 166. Bell Pull. *Jeanne Jarvis.*

Photo 167. Weaving and macramé. *Carol Bitner.*

Photo 168. Little Purse. Among the heirlooms of the Penner family is a blue-and-white huck fingertip towel from Germany. It is embroidered with reindeer and plant forms. Hannelies Penner modified the folk art motifs and interpreted them in macramé, using vertical and horizontal double half-hitches, or the Cavandoli method of knotting. *Hannelies Penner.*

Photo 169. Macramé Fringe with Beads. Greatly enlarged close-up. Courtesy, *Smithsonian Institution.*

Photo 170. Macramé Lace. These dainty medallions are made with fine linen thread and are about 3" high and 1fi" across. Courtesy, *Smithsonian Institution, Washington, D.C.*

Photo 171. Detail of a shirt with macramé fringes. *Carol Bitner.*

Photo 172. "Fancy Ropework" done by Captain John Shickell of the Bal Clutha, now at San Francisco Maritime Museum. Courtesy, Chesapeake Bay Maritime Museum.

Photo 173. "Picnic: Sundae". *Ed Bing Lee.* From the collection of Dr. Robert M. Koeser. Photographed by Peter Groesbeck.

Bibliography

Macramé Techniques

Anchor Manual of Needlework, 3rd ed. Newton Centre, Mass.: Charles T. Branford Company, 1968.

de Dillmont, Thérese, *Encyclopedia of Needlework*. Mulhouse, France, D.M.C., n.d.

Harvey, Virginia I., *Macramé: The Art of Creative Knotting*, New York: Van Nostrand Reinhold Company, 1967.

Nuova Enciclopedia Dei Lavori Femminili. Milan, Italy: Edizione Mani de Fata, n.d.

Paque, Joan Michaels, *Visual Instructional Macramé*. Privately printed, 1971.

Phillips, Mary Walker, *Step by Step Macramé*. New York: Golden Press, 1970.

West, Virginia M., *Finishing Touches for the Handweaver*. Newton Centre, Mass.: Charles T. Branford Company, 1968.

Twining

Birrell, Verla, *The Textile Arts*. New York: Harper & Row, 1959.

Harvey, Virginia I., and Tidball, Harriet, *Weft Twining*. Lansing, Mich.: Shuttle Craft Guild, 1969.

Spencer, Elsie H., and Orwoll, Joanne, *Twining*, vol. 4-65. Shelby, N.C.: 1965.

For Ideas on Frame Loom Weaving

Wilson, Jean, *Weaving Is for Anyone*. New York: Von Nostrand Reinhold Company, 1967.

Znamierowski, Nell, *Step by Step Weaving*. New York: Golden Press, 1967.

Historical

Ashley, Clifford W., *Ashley Book of Knots*. New York: Doubleday & Company, 1944.

Caulfield, S. F. A., and Saward, Blanche C., *Dictionary of Needlework*, 2nd ed. London: L. Upcott Gill, 1885.

de Brazza, Cora A. Slocomb, *A Guide to Old and New Lace in Italy Exhibited at Chicago, 1893*. Chicago: W. B. Conkey Company, 1893.

Groves, Sylvia, *The History of Needlework Tools and Accessories*, 2nd ed. New York: Hamlyn House, 1968.

Jackson, Mrs. F. Neville, *A History of Hand Made Lace*. New York: Scribners, 1900.

Jourdain, M., *History of Lace*. England: B. T. Batsford, 1908.

Lawrence, Cyrus, *Quipus and Witches' Knots*. Kansas: University of Kansas Press, 1967.

Lowes, Emily Leigh, *Chats on Old Lace and Needlework*. London: T. Fisher Unwin, 1908.

May, Florence Lewis, *Hispanic Lace and Lace Making*. New York: Hispanic Society of America, 1939.

Palliser, Fanny Bury, *History of Lace*. London: Sampson Low, 1875.

Ricci, Elisa, *Old Italian Lace*, vol. 1. Philadelphia: J. B. Lippincot, 1913.

Schuette, Marie, "Technique and Origin of Lace - History of Lace," *Ciba Review* (April 1949), No. 73, Basle, Switzerland.

Wharton, Edith, *The Age of Innocence*. New York: D. Appleton & Company, 1920.

Index of Artists

Yarn Suppliers

Halcyon Yarns
12 School Street
Bath, Maine 04530

Unicorn Arts and Crafts
1338 Ross Street
Petaluma, California 94954

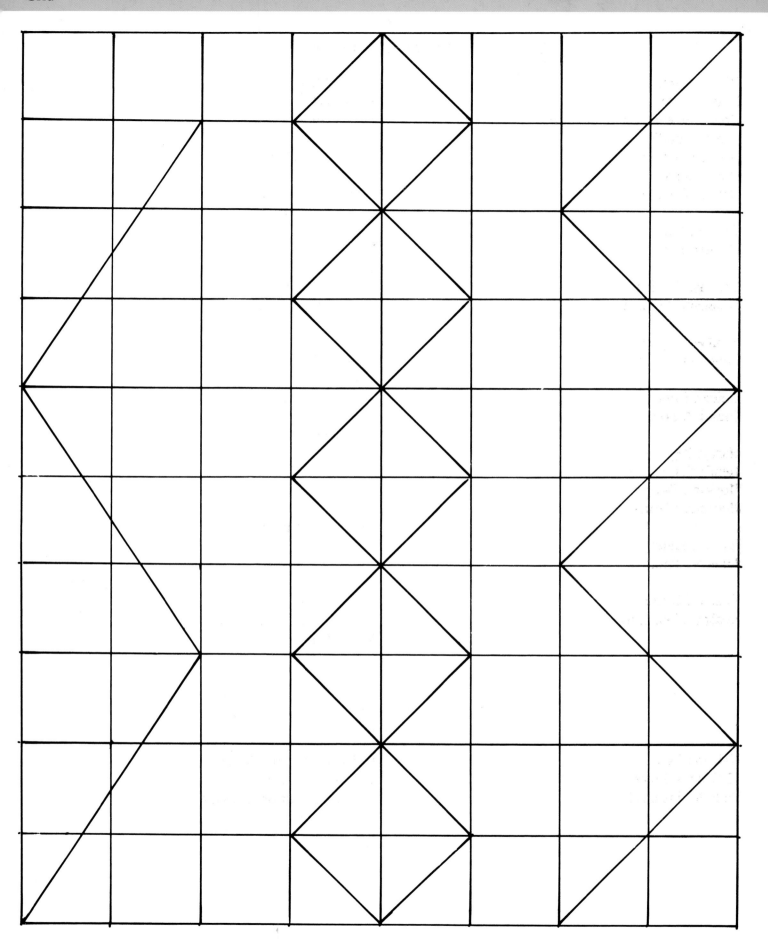

Grid. It's very helpful to have a grid tacked to or drawn directly onto your knotting board. Included on the grid on this page are some of the angles most commonly used in macramé. The straight lines and angles help you to keep your knotting straight.

Half Hitch

Chain Knot

Reversed Double Half Hitch

Josephine Knot

DISCARD